AF412272

COVER: *Freedom and Change* (excerpt) - Lubaina Himid, 1984

ACKNOWLEDGEMENTS

I would like to thank the artists, researchers and curators with whom I have had many meetings and discussions since 2005. In particular, I would like to thank Eddie Chambers, who first spoke to me about key issues in the Blk Art Group more than ten years ago.

The document base and extensive collections at the Iniva Library, as well as at the African-Caribbean, Asian & African Art in Britain Archive, at the University of Arts London, were very useful sources of information for this research project, which also emerged through meetings and discussions. I would also like to thank in particular Sonia Boyce and Paul Goodwin for our intense conversations, as well as Chila Kumari Burman for her generosity.

I owe a great debt to my friend Annabela Tournon for her comments and close reading of my manuscript, which were invaluable, and would also like to acknowledge David Dibosa's ongoing support over the past few years.

Any research project is confronted by the issues that face us in our daily lives, and this work would not have come to fruition without the presence and precious support of all of my family and friends.

Special thanks to the artists who authorised us to reproduce photos of their works: Rasheed Araeen, Sonia Boyce, Eddie Chambers, Jeremy Deller, Lubaina Himid, Claudette Johnson, Alan Kane, Chila Kumari Burman, Sarah Lucas, Keith Piper, Ingrid Pollard, Paul Reas, and the gallery Sadie Coles HQ, London.

I would also like to thanks Charles La Via for is patience and amazing work.

© ÉDITIONS DIS VOIR, 2016

1 CITÉ RIVERIN

75010 PARIS

http://www.disvoir.com

ISBN 978-2-914563-76-5

© photos DR

PRINTING IN EUROPE

WITH THE SUPPORT OF CENTRE NATIONAL DES ARTS PLASTIQUES
MINISTÈRE DE LA CULTURE ET DE LA COMMUNICATION.

BRITISH BLACK ART

DEBATES ON WESTERN ART HISTORY

SOPHIE ORLANDO

translated from French by
CHARLES LA VIA

see our complete catalogue on: http://www.disvoir.com

series edited by

DANIELE RIVIERE

in the same series "visual arts/ essay"

MNEMOSYNE
A HISTORY OF THE ARTS OF MEMORY FROM ANTIQUITY TO CONTEMPORARY MULTIMEDIA CREATION
François Boutonnet

THE IMAGE-MATTER
EMERGING MATERIALS AND IMAGINARY METAMORPHOSIS
Dominique Peysson

THE MUTANT FLESH
FABRICATION OF A POSTHUMAN
Denis Baron

NARRATIVITY: HOW VISUAL ARTS, CINEMA AND LITERATURE ARE TELLING THE WORLD TODAY
René Audet, Claude Romano, Laurence Dreyfus, Carl Therrien, Hugues Marchal

BLACK IS A COLOR: A HISTORY OF AFRICAN AMERICAN ART
Elvan Zabunyan

KEEP THIS SEX OUT OF MY SIGHT
Elvan Zabunyan, Chrystel Besse, Arlette Fontan, Françoise Gaillard, Marie-Joseph Bertini

CONTEMPORARY PRACTICES: ART AS EXPERIENCE
Paul Ardenne, Pascal Beausse, Laurent Goumarre

TECHNO: AN ARTISTIC AND POLITICAL LABORATORY OF THE PRESENT
Michel Gaillot, Jean-Luc Nancy, Michel Maffesoli

SOUND AND THE VISUAL ARTS
Jean-Yves Bosseur

IN FAVOUR OF TODAY'S ART
François Dagognet

To my father (1949-2013)

CONTENTS

PAGE 7: FOREWORD

PAGE 9: INTRODUCTION

PAGE 17: CHAPTER I - BRITISH BLACK ART.

1. MAKING AN ART WORLD: *THE THIN BLACK LINE(S)*, 2011

2. OFFICIAL NARRATIVE: MODERNISM AND MODERNITY—A SOCIAL READING OF ARTISTS

3. THE HEGEMONIC ARTISTIC CANON AND THE EMBLEMATIC WORKS OF BRITISH BLACK ART.

4. FROM SOCIAL TO POSTCOLONIAL CRITICAL RECEPTION: THE EXAMPLE OF *HANDSWORTH SONGS* (1986)

PAGE 43: CHAPTER II - DECONSTRUCTING AND RETHINKING THE POSITIONS OF 20TH CENTURY WESTERN ART.

1. LUBAINA HIMID, *FREEDOM AND CHANGE.* WHAT STATUS CAN BE GIVEN TO PABLO PICASSO'S RETURN TO ORDER IN BLACK FEMINIST ART?

2. EDDIE CHAMBERS, *DESTRUCTION OF THE NATIONAL FRONT*: A DEBATE ON THE ARTISTIC MEDIUM WITHIN AMERICAN MODERNISM.

PAGE 65: CHAPTER III - ARTISTIC TACTICS AND NEW INTERNATIONALISM.

1. RASHEED ARAEEN: THE CRITICAL TURN FROM JHEEL PARK (1974) TO PAKI BASTARD (1977).

2. PORTRAITS OF ARTISTS AS BLACK PERSON

3. CONCEPTUAL SHIFTS AND DECONSTRUCTIONS TACTICS FROM 1980S TO 1990S: SONIA BOYCE VERSUS SARAH LUCAS.

4. THE 1990S: NEW INTERNATIONALISM — A REASSESSMENT OF UNIVERSALISM?

PAGE 94 : CHAPTER IV - POLITICAL CULTURES OF THE BRITISH ARTISTIC SCENES.

1. PUNK POP ROCOCO: BRITISH CULTURAL MOTIFS EMBEDDED IN THE PRACTICES OF CHILA KUMARI BURMAN.

2. SHARED POLITICAL CULTURES FROM "RACE, CLASS, GENDER" TO "BLACKNESS"

3. CHILA KUMARI BURMAN'S CRITIQUE OF *BLACKNESS.*

PAGE 116: CONCLUSION

PAGE 120: BIBLIOGRAPHY

ILLUSTRATIONS

PAGE 8: Fig.1 *Claudette Johnson, I came to dance,* 1982.

PAGE 16: Fig. 2 Lubaina Himid *Thin Black Line(s): Moments and Connections During the 1980s for the Women Artists,* 2011.

PAGE 18: Fig.3 Rasheed Araeen, *How Could One Paint A Self Portrait,* 1978-1979.

PAGE 18: Fig.4 Chila Kumari Burman, *This Is Not Me,* 1992.

PAGE 28: Fig.5 *First National Black Art Convention,* 1982.

PAGE 28: Fig. 6 *Thin Black Line,* 1985.

PAGE 28: Fig.7 *Black Phoenix,* 1978.

PAGE 39: Fig.8 Keith Piper, *Can you Ignore the Fact This Piece Was Created By A Black Man?* 1980.

PAGE 66: Fig.9 Lubaina Himid, *Freedom and Change,* 1984.

PAGE 66: Fig.10 Eddie Chambers, *Destruction of the National Front,* 1979-1980.

PAGE 71: Fig.11 Rasheed Araeen, *Paki Bastard, the Artist as A Black Person,* 1977.

PAGE 71: Fig.12 Sonia Boyce, *Lay Back Keep Quiet and Think of What Made Britain So Great,* 1986.

PAGE 78: Fig.13 Rasheed Araeen, *Jheel Park,* 1974.

PAGE 83: Fig.14 Keith Piper, *Reactionnary suicide: Black Boys Keep Swinging (or Another Nigger Died Today,* 1982.

PAGE 88: Fig.15 Sarah Lucas, *Woman In A Tub,* 2000.

PAGE 88: Fig.16 Sonia Boyce: *Three Legs Stuffed with Hair,* 1995.

PAGE 95: Fig.17 Ingrid Pollard, *Seaside Serie, 1/ 11,* 1989.

PAGE 95: Fig.18 Chila Kumari Burman, *Dad on Ship Arriving in Britain, My Mum and Grandmother, The Three Queens, Ice Cream Van on Freshfiled Beach,* 1995.

PAGE 95: Fig.19 Paul Reas, *Flogging A Dead Horse Serie (Man with a Movie Camera)* 1985-1993.

PAGE 95: Fig.20 Jeremy Deller and Alan Kane, *Folk Archive,* 2005.

PAGE 98: Fig.21 Chila Burman *My Hot Date,* 2013.

FOREWORD

*F*or my generation, born into immigrant families in France around 1980, identity and the political conscience of class, race, sex and gender long emerged outside of the realm of knowledge. My own genealogy is doubly migratory, and reflects two episodes in contemporary European history: the Italian communists who fled from Fascism and the forced departures of the Italian communities that had settled in Tunisia since the 19th century in response to independence and decolonisation movements.

The term 'Black' in British English connotes a political position shared by immigrants and the children of immigrants living in a postcolonial, European territory, and when I first met Eddie Chambers in 2005, just as the 'revolts'[1] were erupting in the Parisian suburbs, I realised this concept could be used to develop a new research project.

This essay is thus a contribution to an intersectional approach to the history of Western art.[2]

[1] The expressions 'revolts in the suburbs' and 'riots in the suburbs' were often used from 2005 to 2015. Yann Moulier Boutang, opted for the first expression in his text *La révolte des banlieues ou les habits nus de la République (Revolts in the suburbs or the naked Republic)*, as did Judith Revel in « Ce que vaut la vie » ("What life is worth"). Issue n° 83 of the journal *Mouvements* was called « Ma cité a craqué, Dix ans après les révoltes urbaines de 2005» ("My neighbourhood exploded: Ten years after the urban revolts of 2005"), 2015, whilst the writers Didier Fassin and Fabien Jobard prefer the term 'riots'. The journal *Commentaire* also used this term as of 2006, in an article by Denis Bachelot, «Voile, laïcité et crise identitaire » (Muslim scarf, secularism and identity crisis), n°114, 2006, p.363-374, as did the journal *Esprit* in an article by Patrick Haenni «La France face à ses musulmans : émeutes, jihadisme et dépolitisation » ("France facing its Muslims: Riots, jihadism and depoliticisation", n°10, 2006, p.112-145.
[2] Fatima Ait Ben Lmadani and Nasima Moujoud, « Peut-on faire de l'intersectionnalité sans les ex-colonisé-e-s?» ("Is Intersectionality possible without the former colonised?", *Mouvements,* La Découverte, n°72, 2012, p.11-21 and Sirma Bilge, "Intersectionality Undone", *Du Bois Review,* 2, 10, 2013, p.405-424.

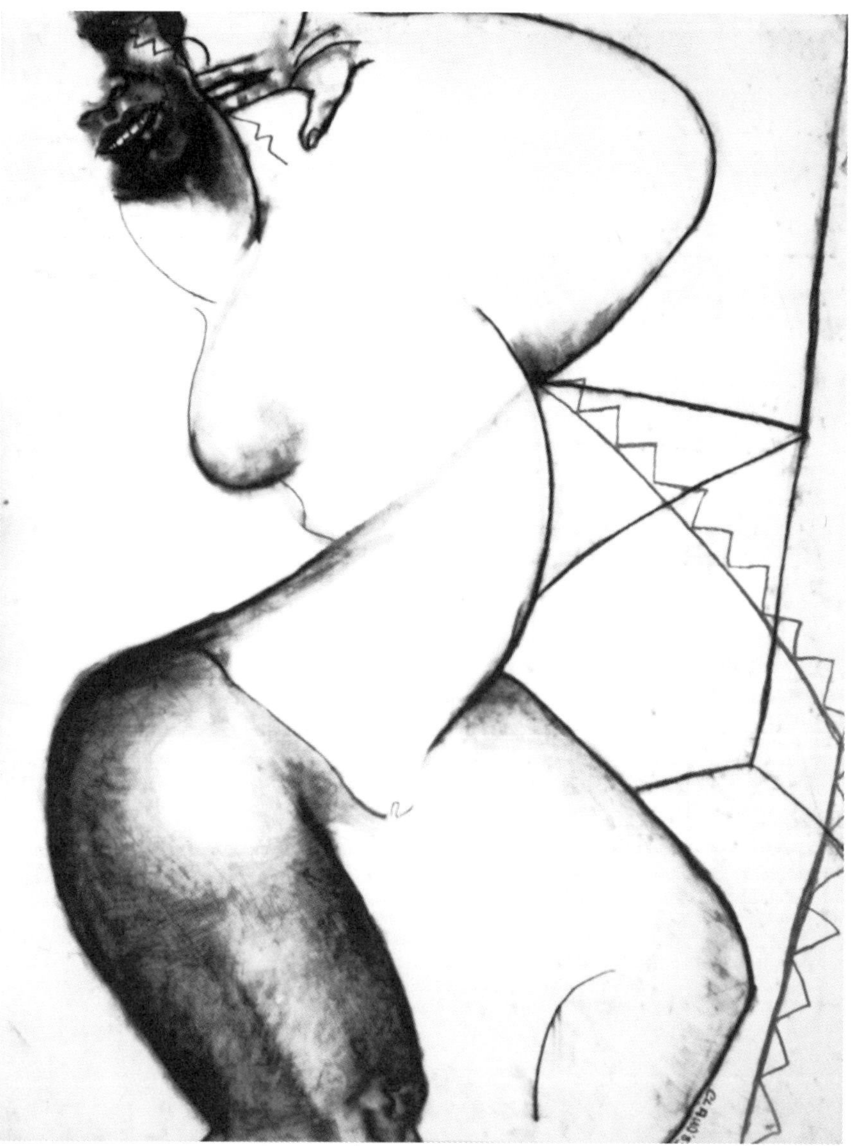

Fig 1 Claudette Johnson, *I came to dance*, 1982.
Drawing, pastel on paper 91,45 x 121, 92 cm

INTRODUCTION

*B*ringing together collectives of visual artists, videographers and photographers, 'Black Arts' developed in Britain in the 1980s. Most of these collectives were created just after the First National Black Art Convention (1982), a major gathering that brought together 'Black' visual artists, but during which no common aesthetic was adopted. Therefore, 'Black' does not designate an ethnicity or colour, but a political place of enunciation that is common to migrants or British people who immigrated.[3] In other words, British Black Art entails individuals who are defined by a common political space that is linked to the movements of British decolonisation in Africa, Asia and the Caribbean. Some like Eddie Chambers became avant-garde artists through the practice of collage, others like Sonia Boyce were inspired by Mexican Surrealism and took interest in figuration, and in particular in the history of the representation of women, whilst still others engaged in a discussion on the history of forms in relation to famous paintings, as was the case for Lubaina Himid. Video and cinema collectives sought to renew the expressionist aesthetic with an innovative mix of documents, archives and fiction (the Black Audio Film Collective), whilst photographers took interest in Gay and

[3] The field of Black Art in Britain is slowly emerging as an academic field in its own right; however, it is currently based on a variety of terms related to multiple practices and affiliations, and even ideologies within artistic collectives and cultural institutions. For this work, I will therefore use the expression 'British Black Art' to distinguish it from the American model, which is grounded in an ethnic understanding of the term 'Black' and rooted in the history of slavery. Meanwhile, the original sources of British Black Art are in the migratory history linked to the decolonisation of the Commonwealth.

Lesbian politics and how it is represented (Rotimi-Fani Kayode and Sunil Gupta). There were numerous shows, but artists were generally given a rude welcome, especially in 1989 just after the Hayward Gallery's *The Other Story* exhibition, which was organised by Rasheed Araeen, an artist and the editor of the art journal *Third Text*. These artists were labelled the 'Angry Young Black' in reference to the realist writers of the 1950s, 'the angry young men',[4] who had been criticised for engaging more in social satire than in a formal approach to literature.

The 1950s and 1960s had seen the emergence of modern abstract 'cosmopolitan' painters such as Frank Bowling and Aubrey Williams, then kinetic artists like Li Yuan Chia, and the visual artist and performer David Medalla, who were part of artistic internationalism. In the late 1970s and early 1980s, art moved in different directions. On the one hand, due to the sudden institutional marginalisation of these internationalist artists, who as a result left for the United States; and on the other, due to the birth of British Black Art—a movement bringing together different collectives and individuals. This movement was empowered by artists who were caught up in a crisis of cultural identity and the rise of racism, and whose practices made use of the tools of Western art, but were opposed to the British aesthetics dominated in particular by the conceptual 'Art and Language' approach (and Victor Burgin's work).

The conditions in which the artwork of British Black art emerged are linked to a social and political history, and in particular the uprisings in Handsworth, Brixton and Toxteth in the early 1980s, in a context marked by Thatcher's anti-immigration politics. However, these productions must be read and analysed not as prime examples

---

[4] John Osborne's play *Look Back in Anger,* which played at the Royal Court Theatre in 1956, caused an uproar in the press, which was interested in the realism characterising the narrative of the hero Jimmy Porter, who was from the working class. The following year, John Braine published *Room at the Top,* in which the hero Joe Lampton tries to rise up into the middle-class society of Bradford. In 1959, Allan Sillitoe conjured up images of rural, working class England in *Saturday Night and Sunday Morning.*

of the conditions of production or of those who represent this history of the communities that emerged after the British decolonisation, as has often been the case, but above all as singular visual and formal propositions, which have participated in and catalysed art history itself.

Long excluded from art history by the mechanisms that construct art history in general and British art history in particular, the artists associated with British Black Art have gained a certain amount of institutional visibility since the early 2000s. The first major academic event that contributed to this visibility was the publication in 2005 of the work *Shades of Black: Assembling Black Art in 1980s Britain,*[5] which included essays, a portfolio, and the proceedings of a symposium organised by David A. Bailey, Ian Baucom and Sonia Boyce at Duke University in 2001. This work analyses the pluralistic positions within this artistic movement. It indicates the urgent need to engage in a critical analysis of these works of art, and to move beyond, on the one hand, the sociological analysis of the conditions in which the movement emerged; and on the other, the efforts in terms of documentation and archiving undertaken since the end of the 1980s by those involved in this movement. *The Blk Art Group* exhibition at the Graves Gallery in Sheffield (2011-2012), and three projects at Tate Britain: The *Thin Black Line(s)* exhibition at the Tate Britain, organised by Lubaina Himid and Paul Goodwin in 2012, the collective *Migrations* exhibition, and the rehang of the permanent collections in 2012 directed by Penelope Curtis, rehabilitated and highlighted the key works created by this movement, from a historical point of view, but not from the perspective of the critical issues raised by these works. Likewise, the recent books *Black Artists in British Art* and *Things Done Change,* by Chambers, who founded the Blk Art Group and is a curator and professor of African Diaspora art history at the University of Texas, provide very precise documentation on the

[5] David A. Bailey, Ian Baucom, Sonia Boyce, *Shades of Black: Assembling Black Art in 1980s Britain*, Durham, Duke University Press, Iniva, Aavaa, 2005.

history of practices, as well as an analysis of institutional mechanisms.[6] His different works strive to reconstruct a historical narrative, collect archives, describe events, and show the groups and collectives that have contributed to this heterogeneous movement. Yet they make no mention of the critical potential of the works within the history of Western art.

The reasons behind the marginalisation of the British Black Art movement are largely based on the racism inherent in cultural institutions as Rasheed Araeen, Chambers, and Richard Hylton have argued since the 1980s. Leon Wainwright[7] has also highlighted the way in which questions on the 'canons of art' have had little effect on the re-writing of the history of Caribbean and postcolonial art in the UK. In addition to highlighting the need to reread the artistic canons[8], my book also shows that the artistic choices made in certain works by British Black artists, and what they say about art history and the history of ideas have also led to their marginalisation.

My book is an analysis of the critical underpinnings of some works that have become emblematic of British Black Art, and especially the ways in which they act within Western art history. In a period of art that is supposedly anti-theoretical, provocative and highly mediatised, and represented by the likes of Damien Hirst, Tracey Emin and other Young British Artists supported by the gallery owner Jay Joplin and the advertising executive Charles Saatchi, Black British artists, who are rarely represented by commercial galleries, sometimes collected by institutions (the Arts Council), and whose work is often wrongly labelled too categorically (and on the basis of identity-related criteria) as 'ethnic art,' propose a veritable critique of the history of Western art.

[6] Eddie Chambers, *Black Artists in British Art: A History since the 1950s,* New York, I.B. Tauris, 2014, and *Things Done Change: The Cultural Politics of Recent Black Artists in Britain,* Amsterdam, New York, Rodopi, 2012. The archival work was initiated by Eddie Chambers with the Aavaa in 1989.
[7] Leon Wainwright, *Time Out: Art and the Transnational Caribbean,* Manchester and New York, Manchester University Press, 2011.
[8] Griselda Pollock, *Differencing the Canon, Feminist Desire and the Writing of Art's Histories,* London, New York, Routledge, 1999, p.3-21.

Many authors—often from the field of sociology that was derived from cultural studies—have contributed to defining the positions of the artists in the British Black Art movement (Stuart Hall, Hazel Carby, Paul Gilroy, Kobena Mercer). Other people involved in the arts, including artists, critics and curators have conducted research on the artistic choices made in the works (Araeen, Jean Ficher, Gilane Tawadros, and Boyce). Among these writers, Gilane Tawadros wrote a fundamental article on the unique position of artists such as Boyce, Himid and Sutapa Biswas, who have a special point of view for observing art history in the postmodern period.[9] My own work opens up new pathways for interpreting these works, based on a historical reassessment of the critical debates that focus on emblematic works of British Black Art to reflect upon their contributions and their inscription within the narratives on art in the context of an art history that is being rewritten,[10] in which the criteria for assessing the works and the methodological tools of art history have been redefined, particularly since 1989.[11] It is organised in four chapters, each of which analyses the relationships between artistic productions and critical theories or art theory, informed principally by the close relations to Black British feminism[12] and new art history[13], as

[9] Gilane Tawadros, "Beyond the Boundary: The Work of Three Women Artists in Britain", *Third Text*, 8/9, 1989, p.121-150.

[10] This essay continues the research undertaken within the scope of my doctoral thesis, *What Makes Britain so Great: Britishness and Contemporary Art from 1979 to 2010 in Britain,* supervised by Philippe Dagen, Paris 1 Panthéon-Sorbonne, and defended in 2010 at the INHA. I was also the editor of *Art et Mondialisation (Art and Globalisation),* an anthology of texts from 1950 to the present, Paris, Centre Pompidou, 2013 and co-editor of the special issue « Globalisée, mondialisée, contemporaines. Pratiques, productions, et écritures de l'art aujourd'hui », *Les Cahiers du Musée national d'art moderne,* n°122, 2012-2013.

[11] The rewriting of art history is commonly associated with the curatorial projects *Magicians of the World* (Paris), *The Other Story* (London), and the *Havana Biennial* (Cuba) 1989, discussed in Chapter 3. It is also the project of new art history. After having worked on cultural transfers, the academic world really took on the project of revising art history in the 2000s within the scope of globalisation, in a debate opposing Global Art History and World Art Studies (James Elkins, Jonathan Harris, Hans Belting and David Summer are some of the principal figures).

[12] Especially the works of Hazel V. Carby and Pratibha Parmar.

[13] Particularly the feminist Griselda Pollock and the Marxist T. J. Clark. See the journal *Block,* and Jonathan Harris, *The New Art History, A Critical Introduction,* London, New York, Routledge, 2001.

places in which Western art history can be critically redefined in relation to issues of gender, social class and race.

The works of the 1970s and 1980s have already been reassessed in numerous curatorial projects that focus on gender, such as *This Will Have Been* by Helen Molesworth and on socio-political contexts, such as *Global Conceptualism* by Luis Camnitzer, Jane Farver and Rachel Weiss.[14]

What are the critical tools proposed by art history to analyse these emblematic works? Whereas cultural studies, Black feminism studies, and then postcolonial and decolonial research have provided critical methodology for analysing the situated subject in colonial space, the methodologies of 20th century art history, which include psychoanalysis, structuralism and formalism, and especially poststructuralism and deconstruction,[15] seem to have been rarely used to evoke the formal specificity of these artistic productions within Western art history of the 1980s and 1990s. Rereading these emblematic works through our eyes today gives rise, however, to methodological tensions: how can we engage in a discourse on the materiality of these works today when we know they were created with the help of tools from cultural studies against a certain Greenbergian formalism? In 2006, Caroline Levine analysed these tensions in the field of literary studies in terms linking the micrological study of a singular text and the macrological study of 'sweeping facts of material social power—gender, race, class, nationalism, colonialism and capitalism'.[16] She developed the idea of creating an analytical

[14] Luis Camnitzer, Jane Farver and Rachel Weiss, *Global Conceptualism: Points of Origin, 1950s-1980s,* New York, Queen Museum of Art, 1999 and Luis Camnitzer, *Conceptualism in Latin American Art,* Austin, University of Texas Press, 2007. Helen Molesworth, "House Work and Art Work", *October,* vol. 92, 2000, p.71-97 and Helen Molesworth, *This Will Have Been, Art, Love & Politics in the 1980s,* New Haven, London, Yale University Press, and Museum of Contemporary Art Chicago, 2012.

[15] Classification proposed by Hal Foster, Rosalind Krauss, Yve-Alain Blois, *Art since 1900, Modernism, Antimodernism, Postmodernism,* London, Thames and Hudson, 2004.

[16] Caroline Levine, "Scarled Up, Writ Small: a Response to Carolyn Dever and Herbert F. Tucker", *Victorian Studies,* vol. 49, n°1, 2006, p.103.

methodology combining Marxist and Foucaultian heritage.[17] In my book, I systematically examine the relationships between the artistic tools specifically used in the artistic productions and how they belong to a place that is gendered, racial, and sexual and inscribed within a social class, combining the formalist heritage of poststructuralism with intersectionality. This methodology enables me to move beyond a sociological reading of artists by engaging in an analysis of artistic forms, while taking account of the historicity of the socially situated construction of academic knowledge and artistic propositions.

My own study makes use of this methodology developing four ways of reading specific works of British art: 1) A study of the British Black Art project in structural and political terms; 2) How the choice of and interplay between the various media used by British Black artists makes sense in terms of art history; 3) The links between the materiality of artistic productions in relation to 'internationalism', through the representation of the 'black artist' subject; 4) An analysis of cultural history taking as its point of departure the racialised and gendered New Left proposed by Stuart Hall and its effects within several art scenes. Each of the chapters and the different readings proposed combine an analysis of the materiality of artworks and an intersectional approach. The readings I propose aim to shed light on the critical content in these works of art—and their position within art history (and within this history, the political sense of the term 'Black')—within the European art world after the end of its grand narratives.

---

[17] Caroline Levine, "Strategic Formalism: Toward a New Method in Cultural studies", *Victorian Studies,* vol. 48, n°4, 2006, p.625-657.

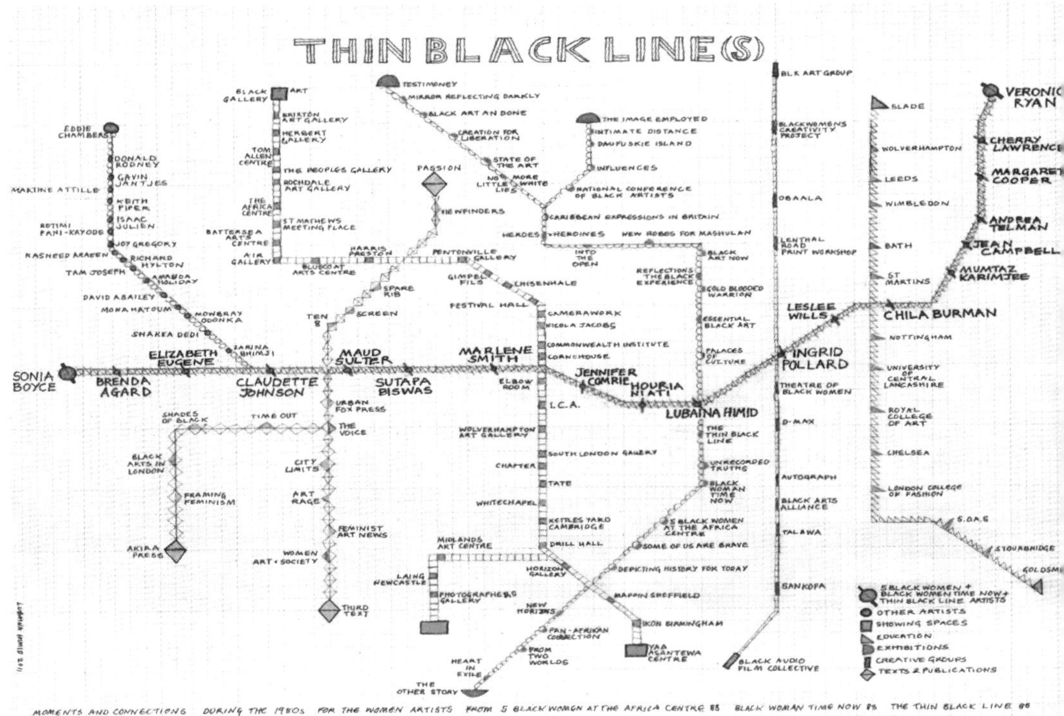

Fig 2 Lubaina Himid *Thin Black Line(s): Moments and Connections During the 1980s for the Women Artists*, Drawing on paper, 2011.

CHAPTER I. BRITISH BLACK ART

What reception was afforded to British Black Art and how could we characterise this work today? Before analysing specific works of art, in this chapter I propose a new definition of British Black Art,[18] which has often been analysed from an institutional perspective or on the basis of a sociological analysis of the waves of immigrants to which these 'Afro-Caribbean and Asian' artists belong. In structural terms, British Black Art is the creation of a discursive space within the British art scene.

MAKING AN ART WORLD: *THE THIN BLACK LINE(S)*, 2011

How can we define British Black Art? It initially took shape as a political project within the British art world. The artist Eddie Chambers was the first person to use the term 'Black Art'. This expression emerged in 1982 at the First National Black Art Convention in Wolverhampton, in the Midlands, a groundbreaking event for Black Art that brought together British, Afro-Caribbean and Asian (Indian) artists who had settled in Britain. According to Araeen:

> *It's important to recognize the role of Asian people in the development of Black consciousness in Britain. It forced the*

---

[18] The artists linked to the Afro-Caribbean and Asian diasporas must be distinguished from 'Black art' or 'British Black Art', the artistic movement born in the 1980s and stemming from the Blk Art Group (1979-1984), the name of the collective that founded the movement.

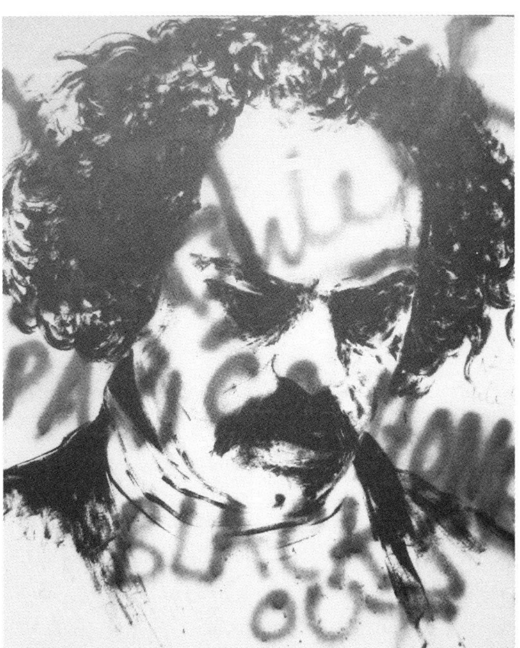

Fig.3 Rasheed Araeen, *How Could One Paint A Self Portrait*,
1978-1979

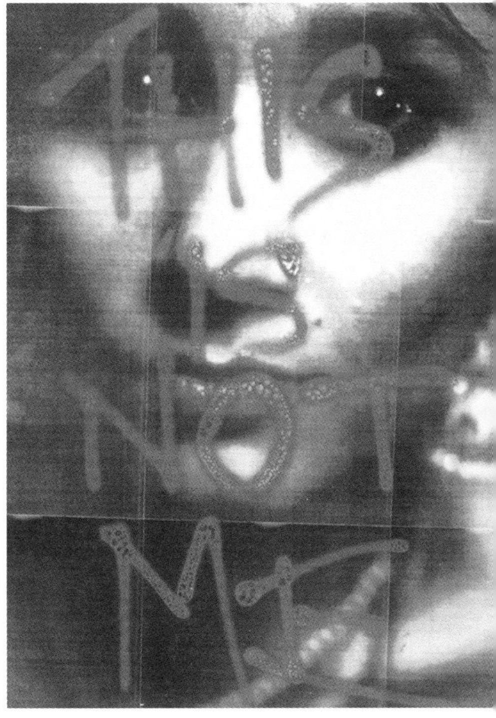

Fig.4 Chila Kumari Burman, *This Is Not Me*,
Laser print and car spray paint 88,9 x 68,58cm, 199

meaning of 'black' to a level whereby it could only be understood ideologically, a shift from the level of visible race and colour to that level which is complex but nevertheless provides us an opening through which the ideas which underpin Eurocentricity could be confronted.[19]

Therefore, the term 'Black' does not define an identity or an ethnicity or even that one belongs to a cultural community. It is rather a political space for artists belonging to minority groups in Britain within which art and art history can be discussed.

British Black Art is a project that emerged in 1982 at the First National Black Art Convention (Fig.5), and was dissolved in 1989, just after the collective exhibition, *The Other Story*, organised by Araeen at the Hayward Gallery, which marked the end of collective undertakings that were eclipsed by personal projects. The First National Black Art Convention was a place in which participants searched for a definition of 'Black Art'. Some held that the term designates a category of ethnic art, others that it constitutes a political stance, still others, a transnational aesthetic.[20] In 1982, the participants at the convention did not agree on the principal objective of the movement: Should an artistic movement be established that corresponded to the nationalism of the Black Power movement, or should the prime objective be to combat racism? Should it be a struggle for the recognition of the contributions made by non-Western artists to international art history? The artists who were influential in the 1950s

[19] Rasheed Araeen, "The Emergence of Black Consciousness in Contemporary Art in Britain: Seventeen Years of Neglected History", *The Essential Black Art*, Chisenhale Gallery, and Black Umbrella, 1988, n. pag.

[20] Some institutions define 'Black art' as 'ethnic art'. The Organisation for Black Art Advancement and Leisure Activities *(OBAALA)* uses the term 'Black' to designate any person of African origins, while for the Creation for Liberation artistic collective, it means 'any person of non-European origins'. susan pui san lok uses the terminology 'Y(B) B(AA) C (YRWBW/M) A', for 'as a Young (Black) British (Anglo-Asian) Chinese (Yellow Red White and Blue Wo/Man) Artist' to point out the contradictory criteria and the inadequacy of ethnic categories. Susan Pui San Lok, "A to Y (Entries for an Inventory of Dented "I"s", *Shades of Black,* op.cit, p. 59-66.

and 60s insisted on their right to engage in artistic practices that were not linked to the political demands made by diaspora communities in Britain. The abstract painter Frank Bowling, who had taken part in the same kind of debates ten years before in New York, argued for the recognition of artists as such and the independent nature of their practices, without what Kobena Mercer, a British professor of African-American Art History at Yale, called the 'burden of representation'[21] by which he means the duty to represent a community. Some artists, mainly from the Blk Art Group of the 1980s spoke about the duty to represent minority groups in Britain, as the Black Power movement had done in the United States.[22] In any case, this event resulted in an explosion of initiatives and artistic collectives that worked with a wide range of media including film, video, photography, collage, drawing, sculpture and painting.

British Black Art is not a Black Aesthetic.[23] The different artists are not united by homogeneous visual research that is common to all of them. On the contrary, the movement is characterised by different kinds of practices, such as the expressionist documentary and *combine painting*, which employs a wide range of media including painting, drawing, performance, video, installation, sculpture and collage.

Painting and collage are the favourite practices of the collective behind the Blk Art Group movement (1979-1984),[24] based in

[21]Kobena Mercer, "Black art and the Burden of Representation", *Third Text,* n°10, 1990, p. 61-78, in particular '*"Representation" concerns not only practices of depiction or textual production, but practices of delegation and substitution such that, at the point of reception, the Black artist is expected to* speak for *the black communities as if she or he were political "representative"*'

[22] Eddie Chambers and Tam Joseph. *The Artpack,* London, Arts Council, 1988, n. pag. '*Whilst artists such as Shakka Dedi and Anum Iyapo were keen to stress that our art should bear witness to, and directly relate to, the material struggles and conditions of Black people, there were other artists such as Frank Bowling who demanded the right to be independent artists –unbridled by considerations of racial consciousness.'*

[23] The expression 'Black Aesthetic' is used by many writers, including Larry Neal and Houston Baker, to designate artistic practices that bear witness to a daily life and culture that are specifically African-American. It was developed within the context of the US Black Arts Movement, which was greatly inspired by Amiri Baraka (LeRoi Jones) in *Black Magic Poetry*, New York, The Bobbs-Merrill Co.,1969.

[24] Eddie Chambers, Keith Piper, Marlene Smith, Donald Rodney, Janet Vernon, Claudette Johnson and Wenda Leslie.

the Midlands in Wolverhampton. Its member artists endeavoured to express the 'black experience', focussing on colonialism, slavery and racism, through the politics shaping the representation of the subject, following the model of Black Art already developed in the United States. This collective has regained visibility with the recent publications of Eddie Chambers (2012, 2014), and also due to the Blk Art Group Research Project, created in 2011 and directed by the artists Marlene Smith and Keith Piper. This group organised an exhibition at the Graves Art Gallery in Sheffield and an international conference, Reframing the Moment, at the University of Wolverhampton (2012). The production of banners, collages, and paintings in a combine painting style, which was described by Kobena Mercer as 'Rich and Mix Aesthetics'[25], can be found in particular in the works of the artists Eddie Chambers, Keith Piper and Donald Rodney.

Many collectives developed in the 1980s, and in particular around the practices of video and cinema. As was the case of Sankofa Film and Video, a production company for short- and medium-length films, founded in 1983 by the artists Isaac Julien, Martina Attille and Maureen Blackwood, Nadine Marsh-Edwards and Robert Crusz, the filmmakers were from technological universities in London known as *polytechnics*.[26] Other groups of independent film and video makers appeared, such as the Retake Film and Video Collective, the first collective that defined itself as Asian British,[27] and which won the British Film Institute Award in 1988. In 1982, the Black Audio Film Collective was born from a collaboration[28] that shook the avant-garde of British cinema. The Black Audio Film Collective and the Sankofa Collective renewed the genre through their aesthetic and

[25] Lecture entitled 'Perforations' delivered by Kobena Mercer at Reframing the Moment: Legacies of the 1982 Blk Art Group Conference held at the University of Wolverhampton on Saturday 27 October 2012, https://vimeo.com/76712100
[26] Key works include *Looking for Langston* by Isaac Julien (1989) and *The Passion of Remembrance* (1986) directed by Maureen Blackwood and Isaac Julien.
[27] Mahmood Jamal, Ahmed Alauddin Jamal, Asad Qureshi, Latif Bahauddeen and Sebastian Shah.
[28] Between John Akomfrah, Reece Auguiste, Edward George, Lina Gopaul, Avril Johnson, David Lawson and Trevor Mathison in Hackney.

political approach, which blended the theories of Stuart Hall, Homi Bhabha and Paul Gilroy (and the gender and Gay and Lesbian Studies for the second).[29] They had the same will to be independent and differentiate their work as the filmmakers of the 1960s. Reece Auguiste comments on their background as follows: 'We are in many respects a kind of hybrid: we are able to draw from Foucaultian discourse, psychoanalysis, Afro-Caribbean discourse, and colonial and neo-colonial narratives.'[30] The political stances differed from one collective to another, and contrary to the Blk Art Group, the Black Audio Film Collective did not claim to be part of the Pan-African Movement.

During this period, black women artists were building a network to raise awareness about the specific conditions of black women artists in art schools, the representation of the female body throughout the history of art, and also the burden of the dominant teachings of Greenberg, Burgin and John Berger. Female artists like Himid, Boyce, Burman and Pollard were identified with an institutional label, as we can see in the title of exhibitions such as Black Women Time Now at the Battersea Arts Centre.[31] The road taken at that time by most of these artists was paved by their reflections on the history of representation in Western art history. This movement lies within the history of British feminist art, which developed as of the 1970s. The Women's Art Movement and its international agenda breathed new life into the artistic practices of the collective Women's Workshop of the Artists' Union. Likewise, the US artists who were living in London like Mary Kelly and Susan Hiller also participated in the development of a brand of feminist art supported by the theorists Griselda Pollock and Roszika Parker.[32]

[29] Coco Fusco, *Young British and Black: a monograph on the work of Sankofa Film/Video Collective and Black Audio Film Collective*, Hallwalls/Contemporary Art Center, 1988.
[30] Coco Fusco., op.cit., p.42.
[31] In the 1980s, Himid, just like Harrison, Hiller and Kelly, became a driving force as an artist, and also as a curator. She organised numerous exhibitions in London, the last of which, *The Thin Black Line*, was an outstanding event held at the Institute of Contemporary Arts in 1985.
[32] Griselda Pollock and Roszika Parker, *Framing Feminism: Art and Women's Movement 1970-1985*, London, Pandora Press, 1987. Their work sheds light on the relations between US and British feminist movements.

Meanwhile, as of 1988, Autograph (Association of Black Photographers) focused on issues of desire, aesthetics and the erotic representation of the black male body, as well as homoerotism. Founded by Rotimi Fani-Kayode and Sunil Gupta, Autograph's initial objective was to play a curatorial role, and it worked with journals, art centres and galleries.[33] Other organisations cultivated and participated in the history of British Black Art, such as Panchayat,[34] which was founded in response to the lack of visibility of Asian artists. This association promoted the creations of artists who were working on the question of cultural identity, by organising exhibitions, artist residencies and conferences, and collecting archives at the University of Westminster as of 1997. Through the Black Arts Alliance, the Organisation of Visual Arts (OVA)[35] and the Chinese Arts Centre in Manchester, the Black Art Movement has become more professional, with curatorial projects and the creation of archives such as the African-Caribbean, Asian and African Art in Britain Archive (Aavaa).

However, another way to describe British Black Art, in terms of its development and reception, is as a generator of an art world, as depicted in *Thin Black Line(s): Moments and Connections* (2011) by Lubaina Himid (Fig.2). This drawing on Canson paper lists the artists, artistic institutions, exhibitions, associations and collectives, art schools, journals and significant publications. This map also establishes the interrelations between these different artists, which enabled this movement to develop. The British Black Art movement responded to the necessity to make visible a type of discourse that aimed to question the ambiguous foundations of the philosophy of modernity in western civilisation, particularly in terms of otherness. To accomplish this goal, the movement welcomed not only artists, but also exhibition curators, archivists and gallery owners.

[33] For example, Autograph worked with *Ten 8*, *La Revue noire* (Paris), Photographers' Gallery, Ikon Gallery and the Royal Photographic Gallery.
[34] Panchayat (South-East Asian Arts) was founded by five artists, Allan de Souza, Bhajan Hunjan, Shaheen Merali, Symrath Patti and Shanti Thomas.
[35] Founded by Sunil Gupta in 1992.

Completed in 2011, this drawing demonstrates the capacity of artists to build and maintain a network to circulate their works and make them visible, taking as the starting point the numerous associations of Afro-Caribbean and Asian artists, and in particular by creating art centres like the Black-Art Gallery. Corresponding to what the sociologist Howard S. Becker analyses in his article "Art worlds and social types", British Black Art progressively generated exponents within art centres, art schools and universities. On a graduated sheet of Canson paper, Himid marks the distance between the artists, institutions, and art centres and indicates their respective locations, as if on the map of the London tube. She chose to not represent the entire network, but especially the viewpoint of women artists between 1983 and 1985.

It is significant that most discussions between the artists, just after the First National Black Art Convention, did not concern the artworks, how they were made or their political orientation, but the difficulty of entering cultural institutions, particularly for the young artists from the working class. Today, Himid's drawing does not show us a face or a notion. Rather, it offers us a map that is the construct of a common territory, as if she were cocking a snook at the territory from which this art had been excluded. Her diagram is also an illustration of the geopolitics and artistic strategies at play within the territories of the Black Art movement. The thin black line of women artists crosses and cuts through this entire network. The capacity to 'create a world' and a discursive space by occupying the territory and taking on key positions – curating exhibitions,[36] in the publishing sector, on committees that purchase artworks and advise public art institutions, and sometimes by playing several roles at the same time on the British map – was the centrifugal effect of the British Black Art movement.

The development of the different links between exponents of Black Art was often made possible thanks to the help of associations

[36] As was the case for Chambers, Himid, Burman, Smith and many others.

like the OBAALA (Organisation for Black Arts Advancement and Leisure Activities), which was founded in 1982 and created the Black-Art Gallery in 1983. The OBAALA is an activist association, which promoted international 'blackness' through what is called 'popular art': 'that is an expression that the wide community can recognise and understand'.[37] Community associations were also involved, such as the Creation for Liberation (Race Collective Today) based in Brixton. The creation of collectives was accompanied by the formulation of common definitions of Black Art. They were also formed thanks to the equal opportunity policies adopted by the Great London Council to support anti-racist projects, with, in particular, the commission of artists that would promote the creation of murals in London within the Anti-Racist Mural Project in 1985.

The importance or even pre-eminence afforded to documentation, and subsequently to archives, (instead of a discussion on and collection of particular works), in the development and aftermath of the British Black Art movement must be understood as one of the major steps in its symbolic construction. The archives were considered to be a political space, which enabled a history theretofore neglected to be written and become more visible.

Since the beginning of the movement, artists had accumulated and preserved archives, generated documents, and applied for subsidies to establish an official framework for that history. This had been the case for the Aavaa (African and Asian Visual Artists' Archive), which was founded by Chambers in Bristols in 1989. This conservation of documentation enabled the narrative of British Black Art to be preserved. It was a response to the fear of disappearing that stemmed from the observation of a lack of 'black' artists in modern art history, and from narratives about the symbolic erasure of their artistic productions, as well as rumours concerning their actual

---

[37] Eddie Chambers. *The Artpack,* op.cit..

disappearance.[38] The current dissemination of archives, as those of the Panchayat Collective at the University of Westminster or of the African-Caribbean, Asian and African Art in Britain Archive at the Chelsea College of Art, and the opening of the Black Cultural Archives in London in 2014, concomitant with the debates on funding cuts for the Institute of International Visual Arts, indicate to what an extent the institutionalisation of a collective 'Black' history and the cultural policies for archiving British Black cultures remain important issues today. The archives have sometimes been used as tools for questioning the modernist exhibition space and as an alternative curatorial technique.[39] For instance, Himid's map represents discursive spaces as well as participants. In addition, the exhibition format, catalogue, and art reviews are defined as spaces that produce different forms of writing about art.

However, to a certain extent, this Black Art network has come together at the expense of the works of art themselves, which are hidden away in studios or in the hands of private collectors, and often inaccessible to the public. The needs of the movement as an organisation and the policies enacted to save its narratives have undermined the attention given to the works themselves.[40]

[38] Several rumours have circulated about the disappearance of archives and works. According to Smith, the archives of the Black Art Gallery were discarded. A librarian from the Tate Gallery also spoke to me about the possible disappearance of certain documents, due to the reorganisation of the archives and libraries. Araeen declared in an interview given at the Tate Modern in 2012 that he had noticed the disappearance of a minimalist sculpture just after *The Other Story* exhibition at the Hayward Gallery. I have not yet been able to confirm or infirm these statements.

[39] Julia Ann Paige Abraham shows how the curatorial policies of these exhibitions function as political performances and communication tools, which critique the artistic institution. Julia Ann Paige Abraham, *Transformation and Defiance in the Art Establishment: Mapping the Exhibition of the Blk Art Group (1981-1983)*, University of Birmingam, Sept 2011.

[40] An artistic network and a discursive space were not created over night, but over several decades, thanks in particular to the (too) slow ascent of artists to positions as professors of universities and art schools. Himid, a publicly acknowledged artist who has works in the major British national collections, is a university professor, researcher and exhibition curator. Chambers is a curator, professor at the University of Texas, Austin, researcher, art critic, historian and archivist. Smith is one of the founders of the Blk Art Group, co-organiser of the First National Black Art Convention, curator of the Black-Art Gallery, and has been actively involved with the professor and artist Piper in a study group of the Blk Art Group Research Project since 2012. Boyce is Co-Chair of Black Art and Design at the Chelsea College of Art (with Goodwin), and professor at Middlesex University. The importance

OFFICIAL NARRATIVE: MODERNISM AND MODERNITY — A SOCIAL READING OF ARTISTS

In 1981, the Blk Art Group,[41] which was part of the British Black Art movement, organised its first exhibition *Black Art an 'Done*. Chambers and Piper had met at Wolverhampton Polytechnic. Eric Pemberton, the Director of the Afro-Caribbean Centre of Wolverhampton, encouraged them to form a group of 'Black Artists', and they organised a show at the Wolverhampton Art Gallery in June 1981. The works displayed were collages, based on a visual aesthetic similar to that of activist groups. Encouraged by the success of this initial, self-managed show, the young artists adopted the title *Pan-Afrikan Connection* for eight exhibitions that toured from the Africa Centre in London, in 1982, to the Ikon Gallery in Birmingham, to the Trent Polytechnic in Nottingham and the Herbert Art Gallery and Museum in Coventry in 1983. The objective was to question the hegemony of the 'white middle-class' perspective by proposing an alternative that would bring together 'All people of African descent in a common struggle against colonialism and racism'.[42]

The original impetus for forming a British Black Art movement was directly related to the social and political events of the time. In 1981, the British Prime Minister Margaret Thatcher proposed to define the identity of British citizens by means of the British Nationality Act. During this period, the laws to limit immigration continued to multiply (Immigration Acts, 1962, 1968, 1971, 1988):

> *Ethnic minority groups thus seemed, on the one hand, to be denied the full protection of the state whilst, on the other, the*

(…)afforded to the place of enunciation has been largely confirmed by the entrance of artists within the territories of art. These places of enunciation should not be translated as signs of interdisciplinarity, or even less as a rejection of art as proposed by other movements (for example, Artaud and the Surrealists), but as a conquest of the discursive spaces of art.

[41] It included Chambers, Piper, Dominic Dawes, Andrew Hazel and Ian Palmer.

[42] Keith Piper created this document (consulted in 2011) in the framework of the Blk Art Group Research Project. The events presented research by Chambers, Claudette Johnson, Piper, Donald Rodney, Dominic Dawes, Wenda Leslie, and Ian Palmer (http://www.blkartgroup.info/index.html).

Fig 6 Thin Black Line, exhibition catalog, ICA,
London, 1985.

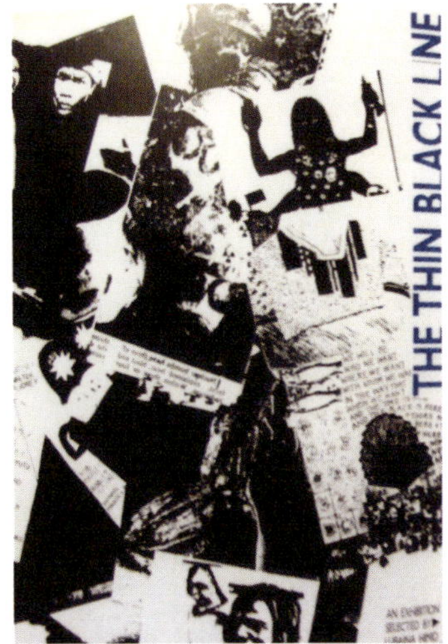

Fig.5 First National Black Art Convention,
Poster, October, 1982.

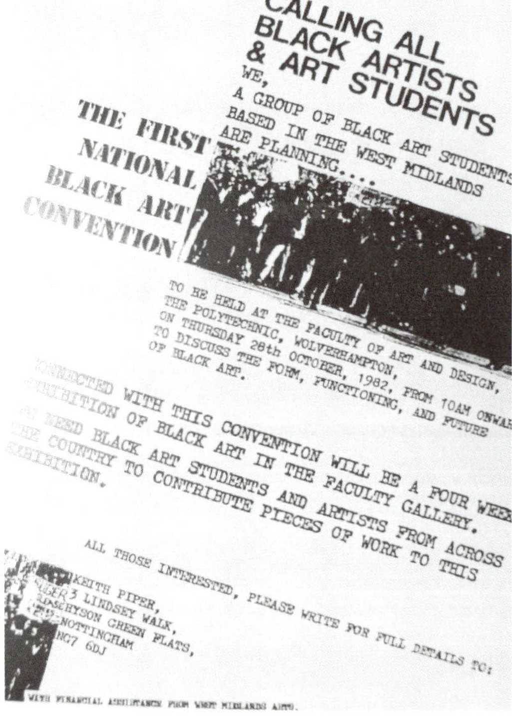

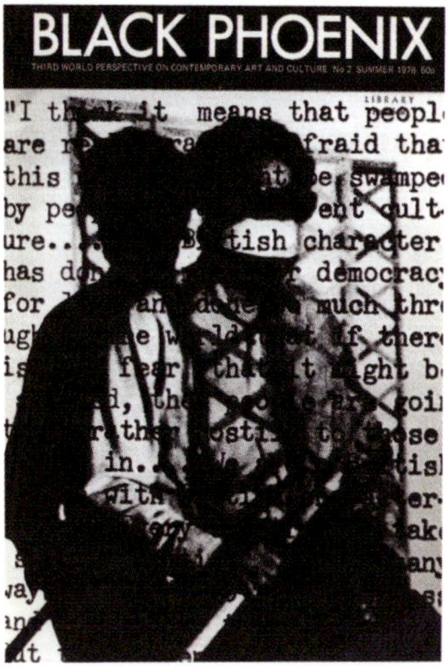

Fig.7 Black Phoenix: Third World
Perspective on Contemporary Art and Culture, n°2, 1978

citizenship of those not born in Britain was challenged. Part of the resistance to this double jeopardy was the proclamation of a 'Black' identity, in which the term 'Black' signified unity in struggle rather than skin colour.[43]

29 revolts were reported between 1980 and 1981, in Bristol, Brixton, and Liverpool, and in April 1981, 110 agents of the Special Patrol Group were sent to Brixton. The name of this operation, Swamp 81, alludes to the notion that the country was being 'swamped by people with a different culture' as Thatcher put it.[44] Additional officers were dispatched into Cheshire, Lancashire and Greater Manchester, increasing the number of police officers mobilised there to 4,000. However, the uprising continued. Tensions also surfaced in 1981 between the police and people in the inner-city area of Toxteth in Liverpool in Bristol (1980), and in Handsworth in Birmingham in 1985. The demonstrations and demands made were referred to as 'revolts' and 'battles' by the media, which considerably racialised the debates. The black communities were labelled as 'problematic', or even as 'criminals' (Van Dijk).[45] In addition, violence was on the rise as seen in the attacks by hooligans and skinheads, and the development of 'Paki bashing'. The laws against immigration and the urban riots exacerbated the tense relationships between minority communities and the government. At that time, the British Black Art movement was presented by institutions (and claimed to be by artists) as a response to the political debates in Britain about reclaiming its national identity.

Numerous exhibitions were held[46] (most often organised by exponents of British Black Art), yet the Blk Art Group occupies a very

[43] Christine F. Collette and Keith Laybourn (eds.), *Modern Britain since 1979*, London, New York, I. E. Tauris, 2003, p. 246.

[44] Margaret Thatcher, Televised interview in Grenada, *World in Action Programme*, 1978, Margaret Thatcher Foundation, Speech and Other Statements, *'People are really rather afraid that this country might be rather swamped by people with a different culture ... The British character has done so much for democracy, for law, and done so much throughout the world, that if there is any fear that it might be swamped, people are going to react and be rather hostile to those coming in.'*

[45] Teun A. Van Dijk, *Race, riots and the press: an analysis of editorials in the British press about the 1985 disorders*, International Communication Gazette, vol.43, n°3, 1989, p. 229-253.

[46] Melanie Keen and Elisabeth Ward, (eds): *Recordings: A Select Bibliography of Contemporary African, Afro-Caribbean and Asian British Art,* London, Iniva/Chelsea College of Art and Design, 1996.

marginal position in the narratives on art written between that period of time and today. The reasons behind this marginalisation have been extensively studied and clearly analysed by Richard Hylton (*The Nature of the Beast,* 2007) and Eddie Chambers (*Things Done Change,* 2012), based on the arguments already advanced by Rasheed Araeen in *Making Myself Visible* (1984)[47] of a conjunction between what he qualifies as the latent racism within institutions and the consequences of cultural diversity policies. As a result, very few or no works by British Black artists were included in general British art history before the early 2000s.[48]

A social reading of artistic productions based on the personal trajectories of the artists, or what is called the 'black British experience' came to dominance at this time. This official narrative[49] emerged from the extreme focus of artists, curators and cultural institutions on the historical moment at which these practices were developed and from the identity policies supported by the Arts Council and the Great London Council to promote ethnic diversity. It also stemmed from the lack of critical attention given to these works, because art critics mainly attached importance to the political and social issues they represented, based on an analysis of the titles of the works and the names of the collectives and exhibitions, rather than on a study of how the works were created.

An aura was created particularly around a talk given by Stuart Hall in 2004, in which he defined the generations of waves of immigrants in terms of the position they took with respect to modernism.

[47] Rasheed Araeen, *Making Myself Visible,* London, Kala Press, 1984; Eddie Chambers, *Things Done Change: the Cultural Politics of Recent Black Artists in Britain,* Amsterdam, New York, Rodopi, 2012; Richard Hylton, *The Nature of the Beast: Cultural Diversity and the Visual Arts Sector. A Study of Policies, Initiatives and Attitudes 1976-2006*, Bath, ICIA, 2007.

[48] Gen Doy, *Black Visual Culture: Modernity and Postmodernity,* London, I. B. Tauris, 2000.

[49] The talk "Black Diaspora Artists in Britain: Three 'Moments' in Post-War History" given at the University of East London in 2004, then the article that was written and published in *History Workshop Journal,* as well as the article "Assembling the 1980s: The Deluge and After," published at the beginning of *Shades of Black,* are the pillars of this narrative, not to mention "New ethnicities", a text from 1989 by Stuart Hall produced for the Black Film, British Cinema colloquium organised by Kobena Mercer.[50] Stuart Hall, "Black Diaspora Artists in Britain: Three 'Moments' in Post-war History", *History Workshop Journal,* 2006, p.1-24.

Starting with the different subjects, he proposed a historical segmentation of the migratory movements of populations 'in the history of the black diaspora visual arts in post-war Britain'[50] that corresponded to the decolonisation of the Commonwealth.

The first generation 'of the last colonials', who were born in the 1920s and 30s in the British Empire, and arrived in Britain in the 1950s and 60s,[51] was made up of modern artists who agreed with the universalist definitions and projects of philosophical modernity. The first wave of immigrant artists was defined as modernist and anticolonial, a position that would be impossible to maintain in the following years: 'However, "modern art" was seen by them as an international creed fully consistent with anti-colonialism which was regarded as intrinsic to a modern consciousness.'[52] Hall cites Araeen's modernist stance as an example.[53] Meanwhile, it is the impossibility of introducing this artistic tradition within cultural institutions that blatantly reject it, which according to Hall leads to the second wave. In other words, it is various forms of racial discrimination that generate an art that is 'highly graphic, iconographic art of line and montage, cut-out and collage, image and slogan; the "message", often appearing too pressing, too immediate, too literal, to brook formal delay and breaking instantly into "writing."'[54] This shift has been identified as a break or as a conjunctural shift by Hall, from anti-colonialism to post-colonialism, even if he observes major stylistic differences within this movement.[55] The second wave was thus made up

[50] Stuart Hall, "Black Diaspora Artists in Britain: Three 'Moments' in Post-war History", *History Workshop Journal*, 2000, p.1-24.

[51] The sculptor Ronald Moody and F.N. Souza, Avinash Chandra, Frank Bowling, Aubrey Williams, Donald Locke, Ahmed Parvez, Anwaz Schemza, Balraj Khanna, as well as Rasheed Araeen, David Medalla and Li Yuan Chia.

[52] Stuart Hall, op. cit., p. 5

[53] One could also add the internationalist conceptual artists David Medalla and Li Yuan Chia.

[54] Ibid., p. 8

[55] According to Hall, we must look for the instruments that enabled this rupture in the ways in which cultural identity has been shaped at different moments in history. Firstly, by the essentialist affirmation of black African identities (he takes Bob Marley as an example), then by the heritage of the struggle for civil rights around Black Power in the 1960s, and finally by the history of black politics associated with the crisis of Marxism in the 1970s. The new political conjuncture led to a change in the political instruments used by artists in British Black Art in the 1980s, henceforth turned toward gendered politics.

of artists often born in Great Britain after the Second World War,[56] and it brought together different British Black Art collectives, which were working against this heritage. The third wave in the 1990s was internationalist and entails an analysis of *blackness*: this local political cultural identity had become mass culture. The artists Yinka Shonibare, Chris Ofili and Steve McQueen participated in it. This text, which had become the official narrative, established a fundamental discussion on modernism from a sociological point of view.

The links between artists, migratory waves, and modernism are the underlying issues in Araeen's proposition *The Other Story,* a travelling exhibition narrating a conflicting relationship, which was first shown at the Hayward Gallery in 1989. This artist, editor and curator opened the exhibition catalogue as follows: 'This is a unique story. This is a story that has never been told. Not because there was nobody to tell the story, but because it only existed in fragments, each fragment asserting its own autonomous existence removed from the context of collective history.'[57] That same year, Gilane Tawadros proposed a philosophical analysis of modernism and modernity in the journal *Third Text.*

This reading of modernism by artists was continued at the Shades of Black conference at Duke University in 2001. Kobena Mercer questioned the validity of categories of art based on the biography of the artist when the works themselves were situated in a national or international context. He asked why we should define artists in relation to their personal migratory trajectory or the place in which they produce their art, and how to analyse their works in relation to the categories of art (styles, movements) in Western art history. What tools can enable us to analyse artistic productions and how are these tools situated in a specific place and context, particularly those of European modernism?

[56] Eddie Chambers, Sonia Boyce, Keith Piper, Donald Rodney, Lubaina Himid, Claudette Johnson, Mona Hatoum and Maud Sulter.
[57] Rasheed Araeen, "Introduction: When the Chickens come Home to Roost", in *The Other Story: Afro-Asian Artists in Post-War Britain,* London, South Bank Centre, 1989, p. 9.

Looking at artists from the New Commonwealth era of the 1950s, such as Uzo Egonu, Aubrey Williams, or Francis Newton Souza, one option would be to relate them to a set of originating national or regional traditions in Nigeria, Guyana, or India. However, this nation-state model has obvious limitations, as it would not work for subsequent generations born in Britain. Another option would be to relate artists of diverse ethnic backgrounds to Britishness as their chosen location, their elective context. This approach has the virtue of including artists like David Medalla, Mona Hatoum, or Mitra Tabrizian, thus revealing the cosmopolitan character of post-war Britain. However, the problem remains that British art itself has always had a fairly provincial and tenuous relationship with modernism. The third option, that of an international perspective, seems the most plausible and the most open-ended. But ever since the high modern era of the so-called international style of the 1930s, the price of the ticket to this discourse lies in the erasure of cultural difference as a significant factor of interpretation.[58]

In the following pages, I will not attempt to specifically define the relationship between artists in the Black Art movement and modernism.[59] I will try to analyse the position of some emblematic works from the point of view of current art history, which is being rewritten. To accomplish this goal, I must free myself from an interpretation based on the experience of the black subject as a principal tool for understanding these works, taking instead as my point of departure the critical potential of the works I study within art history and British cultural history. Certain terms will be the subject of great discussion, such as modernity, modernisation and modernism, internationalism and new internationalism, political cultures and cultural transfers.

[58] Kobena Mercer, "Iconography after identity", in *Shades of Black,* op. cit., p.53-54.
[59] An AHRC programme entitled Black Artists and Modernism (UAL/Middlesex University) has been working on this project since June 2015. It is directed by Sonia Boyce, with a team that includes susan pui san lok, David Dibosa, Paul Goodwin, Anjalie Dalal-Clayton, Marlene Smith and myself.

THE HEGEMONIC ARTISTIC CANON AND THE EMBLEMATIC WORKS OF BRITISH BLACK ART.

The near absence of any critical assessment by the mainstream art world when this specific artistic scene was being developed generates difficulties at several levels in any analysis, no longer of the movement itself today, but of the works themselves. On the one hand, few questions were raised about the methodological tools used to analyse the works created within the scope of British Black Art; on the other hand, a reassessment is needed of the status of this artistic corpus in the history of British and Western art, particularly in Europe.

The overdetermination in the sociological analysis of the experience of black populations' situations in the narrative of British Black Art, the inadequate critical reception of the works compared to all of the various British Art worlds, and the heterogeneous nature of the artistic practices have created confusion on the specificity not of the British Black Art movement,[60] but of the works themselves in relation to canonical art history. What formal questions remain unexamined, and why in particular have critics not made use of semiotics or iconology to analyse these works? The critical theories used by artists in British Black Art (cultural studies, feminist studies, French theory, and black studies) were blended together with the choice of a methodology appropriate for reading the works. In other words, these methodologies are often modelled, in turn, on the theories that nourished artists in the British Black Art.[61] How can we interpret these works of art today in terms of their contributions to art history? Instead of considering the theoretical and cultural tools that contributed to their development as a unique methodology for reading

[60] As we will see, 1989 marks the end of 'Black art' as an institutional category, due to the chilly reception given to Araeen's travelling exhibition *The Other Story*.
[61] Gen Doy, *Black Visual Culture,* op.cit., Kwesi Owusu, *Black British Culture and Society,* London, New York, Routledge, 2000. Houston A. Baker, Jr, Manthia Diawara and Ruth H. Lindeborg, *Black British Cultural Studies,* Chicago, London, The University of Chicago Press, 1996.

them, my analysis of these works takes account of these tools as the intrinsic materials that constitute them.

We must first determine the critical potential of the works associated with British Black Art. Some of these works have become representative of British Black Art, such as *Destruction of the National Front* (1979-1980) by Eddie Chambers, Lubaina Himid's *Freedom and Change* (1984), and *Lay Back, Keep Quiet and Think of What Made Britain So Great* (1986) by Sonia Boyce.

Are these works part of a canon? According to Wainwright, belonging to the art 'canon' means occupying a central position. That means occupying the best place, which is the most representative within art history.[62] According to this researcher from The Open University, the canon must be debated not in terms of the inclusion or exclusion of certain artistic corpora, but from the point of view of the very presence of this canon – 'why there is a desire for self-definition'– and of the supposed temporal difference between the region of the Caribbean and Great Britain. In other words, the canon must be re-examined from a transnational point of view, but also in terms of a 'distorted temporality',[63] within the British academy that is searching for a national art history.

The canon is often defined in relation to acquisition policies and the choices made by major British institutions to display different works. Whilst some works were acquired by the Arts Council starting in the 1980s, many works of British Black Art have been added to the Tate Collection since the early 2000s.[64] For example, *Destruction of the National Front* (1978-1980) by Eddie Chambers and Sonia Boyce's *Missionary Position II* (1985) have been hanging in the Tate Britain's permanent collection only since 2015.

[62] Leon Wainwright, "Mutual Temporal Ground", in *Time Out: Art and the transnational Caribbean,* op. cit., p. 86-121.
[63] Ibid., p. 87.
[64] Some examples include Chila Kumari Burman, 2014, Eddie Chambers, 2013, Sonia Boyce, 1987, Lubaina Himid, 1995, 2009, 2014, and Rasheed Araeen, 1995, 2007, 2009-2011.

A set of emblematic works exists nonetheless in a narrative specific to British Black Art, which was constructed in particular through recurrence and therefore the visibility of the artists. Lubaina Himid, Keith Piper, Sonia Boyce, Chila Kumari Burman and Ingrid Pollard were the artists with the most exhibitions in the 1980s on the British Islands.[65] Griselda Pollock remarks that the canon is not only the product of the academic world, it is also created by artists and writers, through their affiliations.[66] Some works would become progressively representative of British Black Art, such as *Destruction of the National Front* by Eddie Chambers, and *Housewives with Steak Knives* (1986) by Sutapa Biswas, within this circle of artists, then within cultural institutions. They become well known partly because of the publications on British Black Art, which give them more than their due. For example, *The Art Pack: A History of Black Artists in Britain,* edited by Chambers and Tam Joseph and Junginda Lamba in 1988, and the catalogue *The Essential Black Art*, stemming from the exhibition held at the Chisenhale Gallery in 1988 in a context in which exhibition catalogues were thin volumes, established the first milestones of a narrative of the significant works. In addition, in the television show 'The State of the Art' (1987), which spoke of international art news, and in the exhibition connected to it, four artists from British Black Art were linked together: Lubaina Himid, Sonia Boyce, Sutapa Biswas and Donald Rodney. Other narratives were written through various exhibitions, such as *From Two Worlds,* organised by Nicolas Serrota at the Whitechapel, and *The Thin Black Line* (Fig.6), proposed by Lubaina Himid on Black Women artists. The debates between the artist-curators Eddie Chambers and Rasheed Araeen recorded in *Third Text*[67] left a mark and conferred additional authority on their two approaches to British Black Art. They both

[65] Melanie Keen and Elizabeth Ward (eds.), op. cit.
[66] Griselda Pollock, *Differencing the Canon,* op.cit.
[67] Rasheed Araeen and Eddie Chambers, "Black Art: a discussion", *Third Text,* vol. 2, n°5, 1988, p. 51-77

contributed to the selection of certain works that were characteristic of a heterogeneous movement, which Chambers identified as a collective struggle to gain visibility for the international black experience, and Araeen as a positioning with regard to modern art from within a common experience of imperialism. Likewise, Araeen tends to highlight a common European cultural history. In the chronology in the catalogue of *The Essential Black Art,* he places the struggles of Black Power and the Women's Movement in the framework of May 1968 and the student revolts in Paris, through discussions in 1971 between himself as an artist (and political activist linked to the Black Panthers movement in 1972-1973) and David Medalla (an artist practicing collaborative art) on the activities linking art and politics in a collective undertaking.[68]

Today, we must differentiate between the conditions in which the movement was created, its institutional history, political debates and the specificity of its historical works, and their current reception. Rather than highlighting the *trajectories of the artists* who participated in the heterogeneous category known as British Black Art, in the following pages my aim is to focus on the *trajectories of certain works* within British Black Art, based on the critical debates generated by each of them. It was not possible to work on all of the emblematic works, and my objective was not to define a canon, but rather to designate the canon as an initial counterpoint for my analysis of the different positions of the works vis-à-vis 20th century Western art history and their dialogue with the history of ideas.

[68] The works chosen for this exhibition highlight an artistic internationalism based on the struggles against imperialism in post-colonial worlds. Mona Hatoum presented *Under Siege* (1982), a video of resistance showing a body trapped in mud for seven hours, miming the bodies of civilians caught in a stranglehold in the civil war in Lebanon. *The First American Target* by Gavin Jantjes (1974) critiques the politics of oppression against Native Americans based on a work by Jasper Johns. Araeen criticises the Eurocentric and imperialist perspective of the art historian Kenneth Clark in his show Civilisation: A Personal View by Kenneth Clark, a 13-part television series first broadcast on BBC2 in 1969, which presents works by Araeen, Sutapa Biswas, Sonia Boyce, Eddie Chambers, Lubaina Himid and Keith Piper.

FROM SOCIAL TO POSTCOLONIAL CRITICAL RECEPTION: THE EXAMPLE OF *HANDSWORTH SONGS* (1986)

The Black Audio Film Collective's video *Handsworth Songs* (1986) is one of the works that became representative of a social narrative of British Black Art, but it is now interpreted within a postcolonial reading of art. The critical trajectory of *Handsworth Songs* is very illuminating in terms of the issues relating to reception in the 1980s and then in the 2000s. As Araeen stressed in his article "The Artist as a post-colonial subject and this individual's journey towards the centre",[69] works of British Black Art are now being reread through the prism of postcolonialism. At that time, one of the international representatives of British Black Art was the Black Audio Film Collective (1982-1998). At the outset, this collective was greatly supported by Stuart Hall and Kobena Mercer, and it tended to define itself in terms of being part of *cultural studies* and by its reaction to the riots in Great Britain.

This video combines images of the confrontations between local populations and police officers in Handsworth in 1985, how they were represented in the media, and the works of artists from British Black Art. The dispute over a parking ticket between a young black man and a police officer degenerated into three nights of rioting in September. Three hundred people joined the uprising due to their feeling of injustice. This event would be represented by the media as an example of petty crime, and the neighbourhood as a place in which there were tensions, but with no need for further investigations into the social issues there or the living conditions of the local populations. The *Guardian* and the *Daily Mail* depicted the event as a sign of ethnic crimes; however, they did not describe the events as a *'race riot'*.[70] According to John Akomfrah, who made the film for Channel 4, this

[69] Rasheed Araeen, "The Artist as a post-colonial subject and this individual's journey towards the centre", in Catherine King (ed.), *Views of Difference: Different Views on Art,* The Open University, Yale University, London, 1999, p. 231-255.
[70] Jed Fazakarley, "Racism 'Old' and 'New' at Handsworth, 1985", in *University of Sussex Journal of Contemporary History,* n°13, 2009-2010, p. 3.

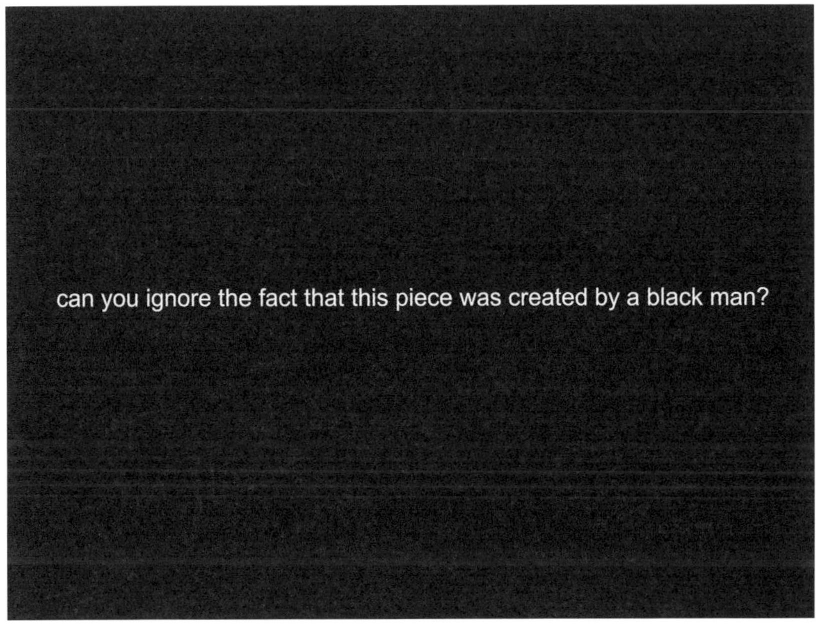

Fig.8 Keith Piper, *Can you Ignore the Fact This Piece Was Created By A Black Man ?* Letraset and black acrylic paint on hardboard, 1980.

piece is the result of a conjunction between the First National Black Art Convention, theoretical developments resulting in new documentary practices, and the rise of racism. It also provides evidence of the links between the film collective and Stuart Hall's sociological theories. Whilst the revolts in Brixton and Toxteth in 1981 had been a driving force behind the Blk Art group, the revolts in Birmingham in 1985 provided the occasion to film and put into practice the analyses developed just after the 1981 riots by Stuart Hall and the CCCS. *Handsworth Songs* is the result of the close affinity between these sociology students and the development of cultural studies at that time by Stuart Hall. In 1972, Hall co-edited *Policing the Crisis,*[71] a collection of articles that illustrate the criminalisation of black populations in how they are represented by the media in Great Britain. What narrative does *Handsworth Songs* write within Black Art? *Handsworth Songs* shows the gap between a private archive— that of the experience of migration in post-war Great Britain—, and the construction of the official public archive, which is often constructed by television and becomes its property. The result is a work of textures, sounds, voices and montage. The objective was to put an end to the search for ethnographic authenticity inherent in how minority populations were represented in films and on television, and to the discourse of victimisation, in order to create a new documentary form that would draw on collage and expressionism. *Handsworth Songs* incorporates non-narrative sequences within a documentary. The camera circulates in an abstract black space that frames photographs and paintings. These breaks act like moments of suspension of the document and thought in the archive, but also as spaces for shows and exhibitions within the film. These inlays constitute self-reflexive moments on the status of the medium, and bear witness to a reflection on the positions from which we speak: Who is speaking and to whom? And especially, how?

[71] Stuart Hall, Chas Critcher, Tony Jeffeerson, John Clarke and Brian Roberts (eds), *Policing the Crisis: Mugging, the State and Law and Order,* London, the Macmillian Press, 1978.

In 1988, this work was read as the emergence of debates on 'race and ethnicity in film and television during the 80s'[72] at the conference Black Film, British Cinema, hosted by the Institute of Contemporary Arts, the very place where these artistic practices were institutionalised. On the contrary, its current critical reception is the proof of a certain distancing from the Western modernist narratives on art composed since 1945, on the one hand, and especially a rejection of the identity politics implemented in the 1980s. The recent renewed visibility of this work is directly linked to its dissemination in the circuit of contemporary art biennials, in particular at Catherine David's *Documenta 10* in 1997, and then *Documenta 11* organised by Okui Enwezor. Indeed, after discovering this piece at *Documenta 11*, the artists Kodwo Eshun and Anjalika Sagar from the Otolith Group decided to showcase the history of this group. In 2007, they organised the travelling exhibition known as *The Ghosts of Songs,* a retrospective of the works of the filmmakers ohn Akomfrah, Lina Gopaul, Reece Auguiste, Avril Johnson, Edward George and Trevor Mathison. In the catalogue, Kodwo Eshun declares that the political project, the question of the recognition and visibility of black people, must not obfuscate the aesthetic role played by this collective. *Handsworth Songs* became a prime example of a new way of making experimental documentary cinema, and the symbol of a break in the 1980s.

Since about 2005, the various strategies for analysing contemporary art scenes on the basis of the globalised art of the 1990s have led to a greater visibility of the practices that brought about the postcolonial shift. For Okui Enwezor, the critical project developed by the Black Audio Film Collective should now be understood within the historical framework of transnationalism. In addition, this work which used to be read within the field of the social sciences is now being read within that of postcolonial contemporary art. The current reception of *Handsworth Songs* does indeed imply a

---

[72] Kobena Mercer, "Recoding Narratives of Race and Nation", in Mercer (et al.), *Black Film, British Cinema,* London, ICA, 1988, p. 4.

certain definition of British Black Art, which is influenced by cinema and video as the place for a return of expressionism within documentary, and also as the expression of the importance of critical concepts produced by cultural studies. On the other hand, it situates the development of a transnational diasporic Black Art in the wake of thoughts developed by deconstruction on knowledge/power relations, which were produced by postcolonial studies.

The reception and the current visibility of *Handsworth Songs* are therefore dependent on the opening up of Western institutions to what is often called the 'globalisation of the arts' of the 1990s and the utilisation of postcolonial vocabulary in biennials and exhibitions. They are also linked to the interest for an extreme plurality of identity positions, including *blackness,* which is represented by artists such as Chris Ofili, Yinka Shonibare and even Isaac Julien, in a vein that is very different from the one explored by the Black Audio Film Collective. It is in light of the changes implemented in the 1990s, and the call to rewrite art history, and within a project to redefine the methodological tools and criteria for evaluating works of art, that I will now situate the critical effect originating British Black Art.

CHAPTER II. DECONSTRUCTING AND RETHINKING THE POSITIONS OF 20TH CENTURY WESTERN ART

In the second chapter, I analyse the way in which certain works 'deconstruct' as this term was defined by poststructuralist philosophers. Whereas critics have largely interpreted Black Art works as those of a realist protest movement, on the contrary, I would like to argue that the break enacted by certain emblematic works such as Freedom and Change *(1984) by Lubaina Himid (Fig.9) and* Destruction of the National Front *(1979-1980) by Eddie Chambers (Fig.10) is based on their artistic research in relation to the stylistic tools of Western art history and on their analysis of the politics of the subject and of the artist-subject within modernisation and modernism. They both assess the opposition between the progressive avant-garde and the pictorial tradition in their own way. Himid works within the notion of a 'return to order', an idea developed between 1918 and 1925, which described a change in approach by Pablo Picasso who was then in opposition to the international avant-garde. Chambers positions himself within the postwar US context to free himself from the opposition between collage and the autonomy of the pictorial medium.*

What does the recurrent term 'anger' designate in the critical reception of artworks? In *City Limits* (1982), Rasheed Araeen evokes an *'angry rhetoric'*.[73] Critics and the media propose to discuss or

[73] Rasheed Araeen, "Paint it Black", *City Limits,* 13-19 August 1982, n. pag.

judge the works in light of the social conflict in which their generation was engaged:

> These drawings and collage reflect much of the bitterness and frustration of young people of West Indian descent which has found more violent expression in Bristol and Brixton. (…) Much of the rest is straightforward agit-prop, promoting black consciousness and quoting and depicting cultural heroes such as Martin Luther King, Huey P. Newton and Bob Marley.[74]

Yvonne Neverson, in *Frontline Magazine,* clearly describes the objective and what was at stake in the exhibition held at the Africa Centre:

> The title 'Pan-Afrikan Connection' was a conscious choice made to recognise three things: the historical dispersion of black people throughout history, the racial injustices experienced by black people throughout the world, to create and develop black culture. All five artists are at art colleges and have consciously rejected the European ideological model of 'art for art's sake' favoured by art institutions.[75]

What consequences would there be on the interpretation of these works if they were no longer assessed in terms of anger or the *artists'* responses to British social history, but as a response of the *works* to Western art history? In reality, as we shall see, neither anger nor rejection are the appropriate terms for describing the relationship of these works, which are deeply rooted in the poststructuralist tools of deconstruction, to history and in particular to the history of modernism and modernity. In 1969, the journal *Screen* was born in Glasgow. It would become the organ of structuralism, publishing articles on semiotics, sociology, and even French psychoanalysis, which were also debated in the French journals *Tel Quel (1960)* and *Les Cahiers du Cinéma* (1951). *Screen* relayed their ideas and published translations of articles by Roland Barthes, Michel Foucault,

[74] Terry Grimley, *Birmingham Post Art Review*, 1981 n. pag.
[75] Yvonne Neverson, "The Pan-Afrikan Connection", *Frontline Magazine,* 1982, n. pag.

Jacques Lacan, Julia Kristeva and Tzvetan Todorov.[76] As of the 1960s, British critical theory took interest in French thought and the *New Left Review* published texts by Louis Althusser, Roland Barthes, Jacques Lacan, Lévi-Strauss and Alain Robbe-Grillet. The feminist intellectuals Laura Mulvey and Mary Kelly were particularly interested in them.

The feminist artists who formed groups after 1982 would specifically highlight the need to debate the characteristics of Western art, which had developed in parallel to a standardisation of the project of modernity, as they did at the First National Black Art Convention. Indeed, whilst history remembers this event only in terms of the impossible definition of 'Black Art' as a common project, which was relayed by the journal *Third Text,*[77] the audio recordings of the conference tell quite a different story. Having long remained in private archives,[78] they show the open opposition of some of the audience to the use of Western art references by exponents of Black Art. For example, when the artist Claudette Johnson, one of the pioneers of the Blk Art Group (Fig.1), explained that her practice focussing on the representation of the body is based in particular on a questioning of the work of Pablo Picasso, the masculine audience contested this idea, while the women artists supported her project. Sonia Boyce explained to me: 'We got up and we left to develop a conference in another part of the building. All around her work, Picasso, modernism, a black women representing herself and speaking about sexuality independent of man...'[79] In addition to drawing attention to the issues concerning gender relations within British Black Art, this

[76] Anaël Lejeune, Olivier Mignon and Raphaël Pirenne, *French Theory and American Art,* Berlin, Sternberg, 2013, p. 20-22.

[77] Rasheed Araeen and Eddie Chambers, "Black Art: a discussion", op. cit.

[78] The renewed public interest for the artists involved, those who participated in this movement, and the institutions became truly visible around 2010, particularly with the publication of *Shades of Black* (in 2007), and after 2011 with the development of the Blk Art Group Research Project by Claudette Johnson, Marlene Smith and Keith Piper, as well as Lubaina Himid's work at the University of Central Lancashire, Sonia Boyce and Paul Goodwin at the Tate Britain and then at the Chelsea College of Arts. The archival work was, however, really initiated by Eddie Chambers with the Aavaa, (African and Asian Visual Artists' Archive) in 1989. Finally, numerous figures such as Gilane Tawadros, Jean Fisher, Kobena Mercer, Keith Piper and many others encouraged a reassessment of the Black Art movement.

[79] My interview of Sonia Boyce, Tooting Broadway, 10 January 2013.

specific conference was also the occasion to make explicit three different tensions between the artists in relation to art history and especially primitivism. First, can the artists in the British Black Art movement refer to primitivism and discuss the position of otherness through the deconstruction of mimesis in representation, as Pablo Picasso and Henri Matisse had proposed, or constitute an autonomous painterly identity in relation to a (local or transnational) blackness? Second, is Black Art a place to pursue the internationalist and universalist project as the abstract modernist artists Aubrey Williams and Franck Bowling suggest, or must artists question the social and political space, or even represent the struggles and demands of minority populations in Great Britain? Third, in which artistic heritage should Black Art be situated: in the revolutionary wake of Dada, in the universalism of abstract art or in the photo-text heritage of Victor Burgin?[80]

It is perhaps not a coincidence that the references to Pablo Picasso aroused such debate a few years before the *Primitivism* exhibition at the MoMA, in New York in 1984, which was the sign of the general interest for this early 20th century movement. Organised by William Rubin, this exhibition alluded to the debt of the exponents of modern art toward African and Oceanic ethnographic art. Jean-Hubert Martin curated the exhibition-response titled *Magicians of the Earth* (1989), which appeared jointly at the Centre Pompidou and La Villette in Paris. In an anthropological survey, he attempted to give equal status to international contemporary productions, based on the (questionable and questioned) idea of the artist-magician. These exhibitions fostered a veritable reflexion on collections and exhibitions and how art history is written just as artistic geography was

[80] This uneasiness vis-à-vis the heritages of art history can be read as a detachment from the discipline, particularly due to the fact that it belonged to a nationalist tradition dating back to the 19th century, and from the application of a universalism, which motivated a refusal to embody it. The silence of critics concerning these works was accompanied by the absence of these artists from art history, in spite of the fact that they were in a movement that had shown itself capable of generating all the basic components of an art world.

expanding. According to Rasheed Araeen, to redefine primitivism at the very moment an ethnic art was developing, which was still labelled 'Black Art' or 'Asian Art' in Great Britain, posits the irremediable existence of institutional racism in the writing of narratives on art. In his article, "From Primitivism to Ethnic Arts",[81] Araeen argues in effect that the production of a category of ethnic art in Great Britain is a neoprimitivism, which is part of British neocolonialism:

> The creation of black functionaries (well-versed in antiracist rhetorics, almost ignorant or mediocre in artistic matters, intellectually timid…), who would speak on the behalf of their respective African, Asian, or Caribbean communities, dealing only with their specific different needs, would do the job. This, in turn would help disfranchise black people in terms of their demands for equal power within the dominant culture or mainstream as they would be turned into *minority* cultural entities. And thus emerges a new 'primitive' within western metropolises, no longer a Freudian unconscious, but physically present within the dominant culture as an exotic, with all the paraphaernalia of grotesque sensuality, vulgar entertainments…[82]

Yet, the construction of an 'otherness' in art cannot be reduced to the primitivism practiced by modern artists, rather it pervades the construction of the representation of the Other from William Hogarth to the present day in British art history. Here Araeen goes beyond an analysis of the history of 'primitivism' to address the general history of European modernities. He shifts from a definition of primitivism as a place in which modern artists appropriated art forms and deconstructed the representations and the mimesis of classical art, to a study of the representations of black populations in art as subjects, and instances of otherness. This confusion between the

[81] Rasheed Araeen, "From Primitivism to Ethnic Arts", in *Third Text,* vol. 1, n° 1, 1987, p. 6-25, republished in Susan Hiller, *The Myth of Primitivism,* London, New York, Routledge, 1991, p.132-150, based on a seminar organised by Susan Hiller in 1985-1986 at the Slade School of Arts (University of London).
[82] Rasheed Araeen, "From Primitivism to Ethnic Arts", in Susan Hiller, *The Myth of Primitivism,* op. cit., p. 148.

representation of the 'subaltern' subject, to use the term employed by Gayatri C. Spivak, the place of the artist (who is not part of the 'white middle class') and the canons of art in the contemporary period are alluded to in British Black Art works, which question art history through a dialogue and a critique of modern art, and American modernism in particular, and through a critical position vis-à-vis the modernist project that emerged from Enlightenment philosophy.

The painter defines a painterly position with the gestures of modernism, including those asserted by Clément Greenberg in *Art and Culture* ("Avant-garde and kitsch"1939), while contesting the the the individualistic and rationalist philosophical project of modernity—with its foundations in the historical construction of Enlightenment philosophy, which include emancipation, revolution, the spirit of the age, and crisis—is distinct from modernisation, a term used in the 1950s by Max Weber to describe the formation of a general model of processes that includes the development of productive forces, the formation of national identities, the rights to participate in politics and the secularisation of values and norms.[83] Artistic Modernism within 1970s and 1980s Britain is often linked to the American model and refers to elements of reflexivity in art, and its autonomy principally within a formalist artistic production. Work remains to be done in terms of definitions of modernism in Great Britain, particularly within art schools, and among British art critics, where the Greenbergian model still dominates many of the current discourses on the past.

For example, Rasheed Araeen situates the writing of universal art history at the crossroads of modernism and the project of modernity:

> The general ideas related to the notion of progress are in fact an integral part of the development of the concept of art history; the concept of a universal art history being synonymous with the

[83] Habermas Jürgen, *Philosophical Discourse of Modernity*, (1985), Cambridge, Polity Press, 1998.

notion of universal progress –of course determined and realized by the West.[84]

Araeen emphasizes the core issues delineating the discussion between artists in the Black Art movement on the basis of two very specific definitions. On the one hand, modernity as a European philosophical project that is imperialistic, progressive and universal; on the other, American modernism. He opposes the minimalism, flatness, and essentialism of abstract art in the European tradition, with the realist and experimental avant-garde in the United States in the mid 1960s—a conceptual art that simply reused the art of Duchamp or the Dadaists.[85]

Lubaina Himid's work constitutes an analysis of the links between modernism, modernity and modernisation: *Freedom and Change* (1984) is a refiguration of Picasso's 1922 painting *Two Women Running on the Beach (The Race).* The artist contextualises and displaces the work of the Spanish painter. Europe with its ancient roots runs towards its future and its modernity. Freedom here is made up of two Venuses. Himid questions the universal nature of modernism, as well as the relationship between the centre and the periphery. She decentres the white subject, which is pushed into the margins. The coast, here, is no longer in Dinard, but that of the slave trade. By placing two black women at the centre of the painting, she calls for a historicization of black peoples, while also suggesting a reflection on sexuality and its representations at a time when there were intense reflections on national identities (Britishness).

'Is her collage of fragments merely a "random cannibalization of all the style of the past"', as Jameson argues (...)? before adding 'Himid situates black women's artistic discourse firmly within

[84]Rasheed Araeen, "From Primitivism to Ethnic Arts", in Susan Hiller, *The Myth of Primitivism,* op. cit,p.140.
[85] Buchloh H.D., "Conceptual Art 1962-1969: From the Aesthetic of administration to the Critique of Institutions, *October,* vol. 55, 1990, p.105-143.

history'[86]: in 1989, Gilane Tawadros defined the work of Lubaina Himid in terms of its postmodern spirit, based on a discussion of texts by Lyotard, Foucault, Jameson, and Habermas, as well as Rosalind Krauss in order to show that the history of black cultural productions must be articulated with Western history, and in particular with the history of European modernity. In "Beyond the Boundary, The Work of Three Black Women Artists in Britain"[87] published in 1989 in the journal *Third Text*, this art critic defines the work of Lubaina Himid, Sonia Boyce and Sutapa Biswas in terms of an articulation between their discussion of primitivism and their break with modernity:

> Where Krauss, Lyotard, Jameson, and others argue that postmodern cultural production marks a break with modernism and modernity, the works of Araeen and other contemporary black artists question whether postmodernism in reality expresses a rupture from the conceptual fabric of Western modernity (and from the structures of Western knowledge as a whole) as well as from the aesthetic configuration of modernism.[88]

For Gilane Tawadros, British Black artists produce works from a specific place of enunciation, which cannot be thought of as being outside the scope of modern European history, the place of a 'double conscience', discussed by the American poet and historian W.E.B Du Bois and the sociologist Paul Gilroy. Thus, the artists' projects 'can be seen to be part of a coherent political and aesthetic strategy based on the interrogation of Western art history *through* history.'[89] *Freedom and Change* is therefore read as a return of history, where poststructuralism had dismissed it, and in light of this history, it makes use of the modernist concepts of authenticity, otherness and race. Coming after Habermas' critique of Max Weber, perhaps we must see

---

[86] Gilane Tawadros, "Beyond the Boundary, the Work of Three Black Women Artists in Britain", op. cit.,p.140.
[87] Ibid., p. 243.
[88] Ibid. p. 251.
[89] Ibid., p. 255.

in the specific position taken by Himid an attack or an interrogation concerning the creation of a homogeneous normative model, the aim of which is less the construction of modern times than their systematic transfer within a process of modernisation in post-war societies. Thus, Lubaina Himid may be responding to this postmodern point of view of the mechanism of modernisation, which has been perceived since 1950 as a closed system. On the other hand, recent studies on the construction of modern times insist on the need to take account of a transnational and interactional dimension in the construction of a European history in modern times.[90] If we consider the works of Lubaina Himid as a historical revision applied to the field of art, *Freedom and Change* can also be read in relation to the historiographic debate in the 1970s about the art of the 1920s, and in particular the 'return to order'.[91] Whilst *Freedom and Change* is an example of artistic research based on a methodology that discusses the position proposed by Picasso in *Two Women Running on the Beach (The Race)*, Lubaina Himid uses Picasso specifically to translate the growing political conservatism in the context of Thatcherite politics. She also uses his work to shed light on the artistic research into 'origins' as well as primitivism for an artist who drew on Ingres' Orientalism, the masks in the museum of ethnographic art, and the Greek art in the Louvre. Himid combines heterodox materials with contemporary practices: painting on wood, wood cutouts and a large canvas hung by clothes pins form an installation. This installation is made up of a pink canvas hung with clothes pins on which she has painted her interpretation of *Two Women Running on the Beach (The Race)*. Two busts of white men are placed to the left of the canvas, and three dogs on leashes are to the right. The two

[90] Christopher Alan Bayly, *La Naissance du monde moderne (1780-1914)*, 2004, Paris, éditions de l'Atelier, 2007. In particular, he challenges postcolonial thought on these questions.

[91] The 'return to order' includes in particular a reading of classicism, and is built against the propositions of the international avant-garde and with the desire to contribute to the idea of a national genius. He derived this expression from a work of essays by Jean Cocteau published in 1926, *Le rappel à l'ordre*.

women are in postures similar to the ones in Picasso's painting, yet there are differences in the painting techniques: the bodies have become brown, the clothes are painted with a knife and a mosaic pattern—in reference to textiles from the Caribbean—floats on their dresses.

It is worth remembering the argument developed by Carlo Ginzburg in "Au-delà de l'exotisme: Picasso et Warburg" (Beyond exoticism: Picasso and Warburg).[92] According to him, *The Young Ladies of Avignon* does not only generate Cubism, from African and Oceanic sources in modern art, rather it is a syncretic artistic solution to representation derived from the tools of the classical art tradition such as the study of proportions, and Picasso's interest for non-Western figuration. Carlo Ginzburg shows that Picasso was conducting research on the proportions of the human body at the same time as he was drawing his roommates in the Iberian style of Gósol when he painted *The Young Ladies of Avignon,* making this painting a formal solution drawing on academic techniques and abstract systems of representation.

By choosing to quote and refigure *Two Women Running on the Beach (The Race),* based on the representation of two black female subjects, Himid is perhaps discussing the flaws in the usual interpretation of Picasso's 'return to order' and Primitivism. Carlo Ginzburg proposes a parallel between Picasso and Aby Warburg according to the principle of a common ability to think of the objects produced by multiple cultures based on their roots in academic art as well as in European literature. According to Ginzburg 'if Picasso was able to appropriate non-European figurative cultures, it is thanks to colonialism'.[93] In other words, by making use of the appropriation of the forms derived from colonial conquests to insert it into formal

[92] Carlo Ginzburg, "Au-delà de l'exotisme : Picasso et Warburg", in *Rapports de force : histoire, rhétorique, preuve,* Paris, Le Seuil,Gallimard, 2003, p.101-116.
[93] Ibid, p. 111 (our translation).

research on the very origins of Western art. This definition of modernism is similar to the one developed by Adrian Piper in *The Logic of Modernism,* published in 1993[94]: European modernism was constructed based on strategies of appropriation not enabling the appropriation of the Other, but of confounding oneself, by pouring our social content into new forms. Formal appropriation thus permits the continual renewal of a social function.

Thus, it is not only this quest for authenticity that makes Primitivism a search for multiple origins,[95] upon which Himid insists, rather it is the ambiguity of the work on the medium, which was central to a decision made by Picasso and other modern masters at the same time to return to Greek, abstract and universal motifs in reference to the project of modernity. A similar comment was made by Jane Bryce in discussing the works of Gavin Jantjes (*Untitled,* 1989) and a painting by Salem Arif (*Inferno Series,* 1975-1981) displayed in the exhibition *The Other Story*:

> An untitled painting by the South African Gavin Jantjes, explicitly points to the modernist borrowings of such artists as Ernst, Klee and Picasso. These unattributed borrowings are part of a tradition of appropriation which includes Aesop's Fables (not seen as Greek); the influence of Islamic poetry in the medieval courtly love tradition, so strenuously denied by Christian commentators; Chaucer's borrowing Boccaccio who borrowed from the Arabian Nights; and Dante's reading of rural Indian folktales, explored in this exhibition in a remarkable series of paintings from the Divine Comedy by Saleem Arif.[96]

The return to figuration is not only a return to the classical (or in this case ancient) model of representation, it also embodies the historicity of the forms taken in their own cultural and social trajectories. On the one hand, *Freedom and Change* analyses the specific situation of black women in the history of representations,

[94] Adrian Piper, "The Logic of Modernism" (1993), *Callaloo,* vol 16 n°3, 1993, p.574-578.
[95] Colin Rhodes, *Primitivism and Modern Art,* London, Thames and Hudson, 1994.
[96] Jane Bryce, "Features", in *Arts Reviews,* 16 January, 1990.

and on the other, it designates the history of *forms* and their cultural transfer from Ancient Greece to the Renaissance, and then to modernism. *Freedom and Change* discusses the way in which the forms embody semantic ambiguity within and through artistic and cultural history by incorporating the history and body of women into this history.

This work can be read as an answer to the major exhibitions showcasing the return of painting, and to the expressionism of the transavant-garde. The former include *Bad Painting* at the New Museum (1978) by Marcia Tucker, a reference to vernacular and popular art, the latter *Aperto 80* by Achille Bonito-Oliva. It is also an installation that extends into space, makes the painting break out of its frame, chooses to paint on wood instead of on the canvas, and places the viewer in a scenic space. Himid explained that 'I trained as a theatre designer and have always been interested in how performance can be an agent for political change',[97] before adding that she also wonders why there is a total lack of black playwrights and actors in the history of European theatre, and how this theatre functions. The materials she used for *Freedom and Change* are exactly the same ones used for making stage scenery: exterior grade plywood and Liquitex acrylic paint mixed with building paint. It is thus legitimate to posit the hypothesis that her work goes well beyond questions concerning only the medium of painting.

A discussion of the iconography in *Freedom and Change* thus requires us to observe a bit more closely the choice of materials found in stage scenery, as well as how bodies are staged in the museum space. The body in performance was the genre chosen by the American feminist artists Adrian Piper, Lynda Benglis and Hannah Wilke in the 1970s. Lubaina Himid shifts the performance from the body of the woman artist (as is the case of the artists cited), towards a staging of theatricalised bodies in a colonial situation. Therefore, it is not the 'performance' of the subject, and of the self, but 'playing a

[97] Letter to me from Lubaina Himid, 28 October 2014.

role' and 'narration' or the acting of bodies in a social space that is central to her work. The association of the ambiguity of forms over time and the staging of the bodies through elements of theatre scenery questions the way in which the bodies represented are impregnated with gestures and postures expressing a relationship of domination and exclusion that resist time. Thus, among the profusion of feminist propositions centred on the performativity of the subject and the staging of colonial positions by means of theatre scenery, Himid short-circuits the established medium of identity-based and gender-based political demands in order to critique the politics of representation and its narrative within history. She thereby puts into play a history and a critique of the artistic medium.

EDDIE CHAMBERS, *DESTRUCTION OF THE NATIONAL FRONT*: A DEBATE ON THE ARTISTIC MEDIUM WITHIN AMERICAN MODERNISM.

The violent rupture enacted by certain works of British Black Art is above all linked to their harsh criticism of the models proposed by art schools in the 1970s-1980s and by extension the canons of Western art history they support. *Destruction of the National Front* is the groundbreaking work of this movement (and not only of the Blk Art Group). Indeed, this work is like a magic key and a reference with respect to which artists would subsequently position themselves.

At the end of the 1970s, the movements for sexual liberation, feminism, and civic rights in the United States opened the debates on identity politics, which were placed at the core of artistic practices in Great Britain. Nevertheless, the discourse on identity politics was already inscribed within conceptual practices, in particular photography and performance. For example, representations of racism were present in works by Victor Burgin *UK77* (1977), Rasheen Araeen, *Paki Bastard* (1977), and Gilbert & George *Cocky Patriot* (1980). The anti-conformist youth in the East End immigrant district in London was represented in *Dirty Words* and *Youth Attack* (1982). Fists are raised, the church is upside down, sex is no longer taboo, and the youth are roaming around in gangs.[98] During this short period of time, the artists in the Blk Art Group positioned themselves in a contradictory stance, opening a 'third space', which was not within the antimodernist rejection of painting or the postmodern conceptual discourse. Kobena Mercer emphasizes the difficulty of choosing to paint at a moment in which conceptual art and photo-text were dominant (1977-1982). Artists were forced to choose between the social art of the photo-text movement, painting considered to be a neoconservative practice, antimodernism and postmodernism.[99]

The resurgence of painting and figuration were perceived at that time as a kind of neoconservatism, a rejection of antimodernism. Kobena Mercer insists on the convergence of this return to painting with the return of the New Right in the aftermath of May 1968. This preference for painting would be considered as over in 1987, due to the conjunction of a conference on British Black cinema and the consecration of Stuart Hall as its mentor, with his famous talk on this occasion entitled "New ethnicities". Indeed, in the late 1980s, film and photography would become the principle tools of the different collectives (Sankofa Film, Black Audio Film, Autograph, and D-Max Collective). Stuart Hall and Kobena Mercer put in place fundamental elements for understanding the Blk Art Group with respect to all the different British Black Art movements. They show that the favourite subject of these artists is the emergence of modernism, but that they chose to position themselves formally speaking in opposition to these narratives, and that they accomplish this aim principally in relation to American artistic practices.

However, the specific positioning of this work vis-à-vis the status of painting and collage at the beginning of the 1980s has not yet been analysed clearly enough. Furthermore, *Destruction of the*

[98] Gilbert & George, *For Aids,* London, Anthony d'Offay Gallery, 1989. With AIDS raging, in 1989 Gilbert & George organised an exhibition in support of Crusaid. This theme was recurrent in the 1990s with series of negatives of blood and urine viewed through a microscope (*Blood On Piss,* 1996).
[99] Kobena Mercer, "Perforations", unpublished conference paper, Wolverhampton, October 2012.

National Front signals that the specific dialogue undertaken by the artists in the Blk Art Group with the United States was not limited to British Black Art, but was constructed as a political and pictorial response to the shift from modern to postmodern literature and art.

When Eddie Chambers organised the exhibition *Black People and the British Flag*[100] (1993), David Hammons' red, black and green flag (1990) chosen for the exhibition, bore the official colours of Marcus Garvey's African Diaspora. This black nationalist American had promoted this flag when he created the UNIA (Universal Negro Improvement Association). He supported the principle of an international African community, rallied in favour of class struggle and proposed a racial theory. Keith Piper and Eddie Chambers, as well as the artist Donald Rodney first drew on the American concept of *blackness*, and they turned toward Marcus Garvey in particular. At the end of the First World War, black activism started to develop: the enlistment of 400,000 blacks in the US army had created a feeling of belonging to the nation, and was a call for the recognition of their civil rights, despite the split by the American Federation of Labour, which was hostile to the mobilisation of black workers. Garvey is the first to have created an independent black nationalist organisation, which would become anti-communist. However, the role and function of the working classes represents one of the first key concerns of the Blk Art Group, as well as anti-imperialism, which Garvey did not defend. Meanwhile, rather than nationalism, it is Africanist thought and notably the diasporic conscience that was of interest to the artists. Eddie Chambers read Larry Neale, Addison Gayle, and *The Black Aesthetics* (1971), as well as Woodie King and *Black Poets and Black Prophets* (1972). In other words, he read authors who demanded the empowerment of Afro-American Literature—more than essentialist politics—a literature based on the specific experiences of black people in the United States. When Eddie Chambers created the Pan-

[100] The exhibition *Black People and the British Flag* brought together 18 artists at the Cornerhouse in Manchester (8 May-13 June 1993), and then at the City Gallery in Leicester.

Afrikan Connection with Keith Piper in 1982, he expressed his explicit desire to unite exponents of the African Diaspora under a common banner. That very same year, he organised the First National Black Art Convention in Wolverhampton. This gathering was similar to the CONFABA (Conference on the Functional Aspect of Black Arts) held in 1968 in Illinois in the United States and the Organization of Black American Culture in Chicago, the previous year, which was supposed to explicitly define a black nationalist conscience.[101] The end of the 1960s in the US would also mean the end of demands for civil rights and the rise of black revolutionary coalitions such as the OBAC (Organization of Black American Culture), which would become Afri-Cobra in Chicago before moving to New York. Then the group Spiral was established, bringing together three black American artists: Romare Bearden, Ernest Crishlow and Norman Lewis. Similarly, the CARD (Campaign Against Racial Discrimination) was created in Great Britain in 1965 on the initiative of Martin Luther King, when Malcom X was spending time in London.[102] In *Blueprint for Black Criticism* (1977), Addison Gayle argues that the artist must promote a 'Black aesthetic' in the United States. He integrates some Marxist ideas into his arguments and explains the tyranny oppressing black people in terms of economic determinism. He supports a plan of action, emancipation and resistance. Numerous artists associated with the Blk Art Group engaged in a dialogue with issues in the United States, including Donald Rodney who criticised in particular the policies targeting Native Americans in *Untitled* (1981), a composition of 14 boxes filled with red, white and blue figurines of Mickey Mouse over which a series of labels narrates the conquest of US territory.

The relationship between the art produced in the United States and Great Britain goes well beyond the specific political

[101] Elvan Zabunyan, *Black Is a Color*, Paris, Dis Voir, 2004, p103.
[102] The 1980s in Great Britain were indelibly marked by Margaret Thatcher, while her counterpart Ronald Reagan was reigning in the United States. The Black Art movement was associated with Black Power in the United States, beginning in 1965 and ending in 1975, and as we have seen, its British counterpart emerged later and came to an end in the 1990s.

demands of American Black Art. It entails a reflection on artistic media within art, which uses pictorial tools that are at the crossroads of the activist flyer and conceptual art. The quadriptych *Destruction of the National Front* presents a British flag painted in the format of a swastika mounted on black card paper, which breaks apart progressively between the first collage and the last. This collage establishes a link between British black culture and the national flag, the Union Jack, but it also establishes a relationship between the practice of collage and painting or neo-dada combine painting. *Destruction of the National Front* can be read in parallel to Jasper Johns' *Target with Plaster Cast* (1955), a large black and yellow target on a red background, above which faces, masks, and moulded body parts are set in boxes. Eddie Chambers rejects figuration, and challenges the white hegemonic politics of representation. Socially invisible, the body disappears. It becomes imperceptible, just like the hero in Ralph Ellison's novel *Invisible Man* (1952),[103] who is invisible in a white society. Paul Gilroy develops this idea in his book entitled *There Ain't no Black in the Union Jack.*[104] However, Chambers tears up these artistic as well as symbolic associations and destroys the composition. The viewer is abandoned, confronted with the ambiguity of a work of art that could be interpreted as lauding modernism or breaking with its history. What should we think of the black monochrome square surface on which the painted collage of the Union Jack is placed? Is it a reference to the history of painting in Malevitch's work or to Ad Reinhardt's *Black Paintings* (*Abstract Painting Black,* 1960-1966)? Furthermore, the black card paper marks the lack of artistic heritage for an entire generation – what Kobena Mercer calls the 'orphans'[105] – who are not operating within the abstract modernism of the Caribbean Artists Movement (1966-1972), as did the abstract artist Aubrey Williams, nor as exponents of

[103] Ralph Ellison, *Invisible Man,* New York, Random House, 1952.
[104] Paul Gilroy, *There Ain't no Black in the Union Jack',* London, Hutchinson, 1987.
[105] Kobena Mercer, "Perforations", op. cit.

internationalist conceptual art, as was the case of David Medalla in the Signals group (1964-1966). The figure of the orphan artist[106] illustrates in particular the breaking away of this generation from a certain language of Western art history, and a return to the Dadaist tradition.

Sonia Boyce proposed a formalist reading of this work, which is representative of the Blk Art Group and Black Art, at the conference held on the anniversary of the First National Black Art Convention in October 2012.[107] She recalled to what extent the British art school disseminated the formalist theories of Clement Greenberg (and Michael Fried) at the end of the 1970s and the beginning of the 1980s: 'This doctrine was the dominant discourse despite the incursions of feminist art, pop art, performance and new media, to name but a few. Art for art's sake, as it colloquially became known, or form and function, was the defining modus operandi within studio practice.'[108] The artist interprets *Destruction of the National Front* as the desire to break with this late universal modernism through the use of collage, one of the first techniques of modernists. She explains how collage and black painting (two phases in modernism) reveal two positions against which this work is defined. On the one hand, the autonomy of the pictorial medium, its flatness; and on the other, collage, the avant-garde, and deconstruction. Emerging from the links between American art and British Black Art, *Destruction of the National Front* enacts the modernism defended by Clément Greenberg and the European avant-garde, which draws on collage and figuration. This work shows us the methodological crux or the type of questions constantly explored by Black Art. It questions the scission inherent in the 20th century between the idea of a universal abstract art, which was proposed by American modernism, and the idea of otherness (proposed by Dadaists in particular, and discussed by Americans in the Harlem Renaissance movement).

[106] Ibid, op. cit.
[107] Most of the talks presented at the Reframing the Moment: Legacies of 1982 Blk Art Group Conference are available at http://www.blkartgroup.info/conferencevid.html
[108] Sonia Boyce, unpublished conference paper, p. 4.

However, the black base is simply a piece of black card paper. In other words, the black card paper is not built *by* paint, as is the case in the paintings by Jasper Johns, and Rauschenberg in his combine paintings. The four pieces of black archival paper, with a format corresponding to the most commonly sold paper, are put at the disposal of collage. Indeed, they come to support painting. Because of an error in the label, the Tate Britain presents the composition of this worked acquired in 2013, as a series of black screenprints.[109] Chambers did indeed work with screenprinting, a medium that uses mechanical reproduction. Following this affiliation, the black background would seem to function as the background of a poster inscribing him in the tradition of poster artists, or in relation to the practices of artists such as Andy Warhol, Roy Lichtenstein and Robert Rauschenberg. The black part partially covers the paper that is in portrait format (82,7 x 239,2 cm). In addition, Eddie Chambers has often insisted on his interest for propaganda posters, which can be seen in several of his antiracist works like *Black British* (1981). Likewise, in the catalogue of the exhibition *Black People and the British Flag,* which Chambers organised at the Institute of the New International Visual Arts in 1993, Lola Young evokes the different symbolic uses of the flag: as the vehicle of racism via the Nazi swastika, as a means of support for patriotism in the publications concerning the first Gulf War in *The Sun*, but also of Britishness, which supposes a transcendence of the specific cultural identities in the daily newspapers that report on the success of athletes like Niger Benn, Frank Bruno, Tessa Anderson. Just as the paper used for newspapers or posters, the blank homogeneous black support in *Destruction of the National Front* conveys a series of constructed social discourses around the Union Jack. As a poststructuralist medium, it bears witness to the linguistic shift in art that occurred in 1968. Eddie Chambers' work on the medium is a way to distance himself from the abstract expressionists, and in this endeavour he is also closer to pop artists.

[109] Eddie Chambers sent a message to the Tate on 19 September 2014 to correct this error, but nothing has yet been done.

Another artist in the Blk Art Group uses a similar 'four panel progressivity'. This time, the canvas (and not the paper) moves beyond the frame and mimes the use of the activist banner. Keith Piper's *The Black Assassin Saint* (1982) also functions as a reflection on the poster and the activist banner. In the following decade, Piper's work on the banner would become the subject studied in the works of Jeremy Deller and Mark Wallinger as the re-utilisation of materials specific to the popular classes in a language accessible to everyone. According to Keith Piper, 'People who aren't versed in modernist language find the gallery undecipherable. It is still the case. It has to do with the activist type of practice, that recognises that the art world speaks in codes.'[110] As Villeglé and Hains understood in the 1960s, the poster and the banner are the visual resources offered by cities in reserved spaces, which are used to announce concerts and other events. In addition, Keith Piper insists on his interest for Robert Rauschenberg, speaking of the use of the canvas, its shape, how it is woven: 'Looking at the Black Assassin Saint, it was a challenge to the large framed painting. It was a way of moving away from the logic of the warehouse, and the whole thing about painting large canvases, as a sign of access to economic power.'[111] This economy of work is also present in his choice of powder paint bought at the Learning Centre, a store for children. This technique permits him to engage in a kind of modest art, in which he can develop his work, hang it with nails and string, then roll it up or fold it and leave with a suitcase.

Eddie Chambers adds a symbol painted with gouache on the black support, which had been used in the Nazi racist discourse. The paper is mounted. This affiliation from Schwitters to the neo-dada model thus describes a context or defines a situation: the mass dissemination of a racist discourse, disguised behind the national flag. If *Destruction of the National Front* is to be situated within post-war American practices, it is more as a foil than as a reference to universalism and to the sublime

[110] Interview with Keith Piper, Islington, 22 April 2015.
[111] Ibid.

of abstract expressionism, more an example of a found object, Arte Povera, or a return to a situated context. The four pieces of black card paper embody a narration, and the acts applied to them generate the story. Whilst the materials used for the work were not found in the street, the act of tearing it up is similar to how Raymond Hains and Jacques Villeglé tore up advertising posters in the French context. The act of ripping up posters is for Villeglé a staunch refusal of situated political content, as in the case of the elections of François Mitterrand in 1981 or his manoeuvrings with the French Communist Party. In other words, it is a comment on and from within the social and political urban space. The artist's body appears in this act of revolt, which is more performative than pictorial, in the physical and visible trace he leaves on the paper. If there is a reference to modernism, it is in the acts he commits. Eddie Chambers thus reinscribes movement less in painting than in collage, and especially in deconstruction, bringing him closer to *French Theory* and in particular the discourse analysis practiced by Michel Foucault and Jacques Derrida's deconstruction.[112]

On the one hand, the work of Lubaina Himid examines postmodernism as the space for a feminist rereading of modern art based on her reflections on the transmission of forms. On the other, Eddie Chambers' work operates within an artistic transnationalism indicating the passage between the art of propaganda and a support used for mass culture, similar to how the collagists in the 1930s were divided between the heirs of Schwitters and those of Heartfield, whose techniques the New Realists appropriated in the 1960s.[113] Whilst the work of Lubaina Himid and Eddie Chambers both insist on the importance of the place of enunciation—Black British feminism for Himid, and transnational pan-Africanism/Marxism for Chambers, it is

[112] The study of the gesture of the artist as a trace of the movement of the body distinguishes this work from that of Sonia Boyce, who also uses the quadriptych format (*Lay Back Keep Quiet and Think of What Made Britain So Great,* 1986) in a narrative approach, which is closer to the use of seriality in painting.
[113] Benjamin Buchloh, "Allegorical Procedures: Appropriation" (1982), version revised in Alexander Alberro and Sabeth Buchmann, *Art After Conceptual Art,* London, Vienna, MIT Press, Generali Foundation, 2006, p.27-52.

less representative of a populist modernism, a black transnationalism, or a pan-Africanism than of a critical posture vis-à-vis the orientations taken by the avant-garde or of an affiliation to its lineage. To enact this critique, both pieces propose a debate on the pictorial medium used, based on two similar strategies of deconstruction, which comment on one practice with another. In both cases, this comment acts by distorting or reversing painting within historically situated contexts.

CHAPTER III. ARTISTIC TACTICS AND NEW INTERNATIONALISM

What do the major breaks and changes in artistic strategies made by the artists Rasheed Araeen and Sonia Boyce reveal? In this chapter, I will focus on the congruence between the political and cultural changes that occurred between 1975 and 1989 and the artistic choices made by these two artists to reassess them in light of the notions of 'cosmopolitism', 'internationalism' and 'new internationalism'.

The radical changes within their artistic practices can be read as a consequence of the social and political transformations that were affecting the very nature of the aesthetic experience. They would express these changes as a kind of disobedience to the art trends, sometimes by breaking with their previous practices, but also by taking positions with respect to the representation of the subject within internationalist art history.

Although he was not active in the British Black Art movement between 1982 and 1989, but more in the previous generation, Araeen is nonetheless one of the key figures of British Black Art, due to his activities as an editor and art critic, and especially the heritage left behind by his works, particularly his performance Paki Bastard (Portrait of the Artist as a Black Person), 1977 (Fig.11). *If* Jheel Park, 1974 (Fig.13) *marked his passage from kinetic art to minimalist universalism, Paki Bastard introduces his return to figuration.*

On the contrary, in the 1990s, the feminist artist Sonia Boyce made a break with her self- portrait paintings Lay Back Keep Quiet and Think of What Made Britain So Great,1986 (Fig.12) *in which she depicted herself as a 'black woman artist' in Great Britain, and turned toward a practice exploring sexual and gendered identities that is more universal with* Three Legs Stuffed with Hair

Fig.9 Lubaina Himid, *Freedom and Change*,
Car paint, wood, acrylic and paper collage on cloth. 275 x 550 cm, 1984.

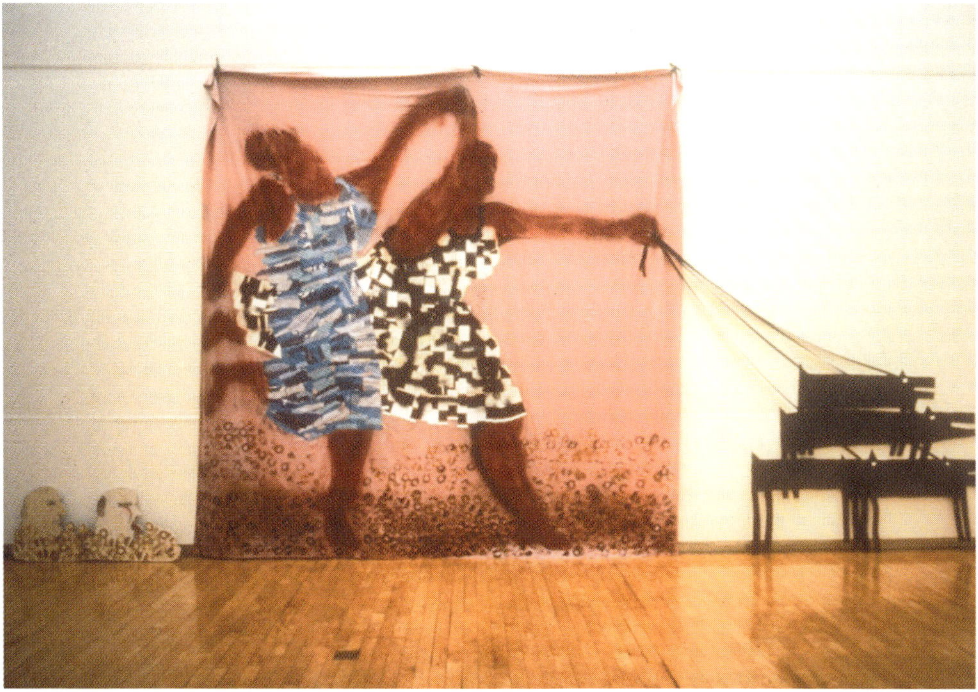

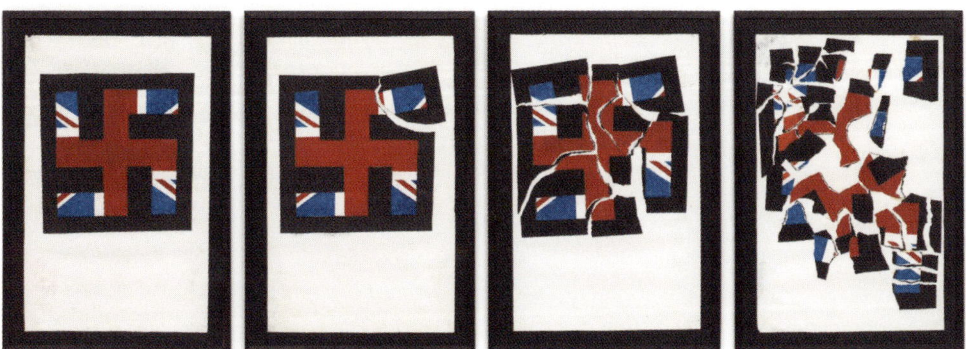

Fig.10 Eddie Chambers, *Destruction of the National Front*,
Collage, 4 pannels, 82,7 x 239,2 cm, 1979-1980.

(1995). Blackness and gender-based identities were also of interest to other artists such as Sarah Lucas.

RASHEED ARAEEN: THE CRITICAL TURN FROM *JHEEL PARK* (1974) TO *PAKI BASTARD* (1977).

The period from 1975 to 1989 was the theatre of political and cultural changes, which included the passage from Fordism to post-Fordism, the rise of conservatism and the breaking up of the left, particularly of Communism. André Gorz published *Farewell to the Working Class,* in which he reflected on how the proletarian class was becoming a minority in a post-industrial society: A neo-proletariat, with no definite social class or job security, which could only aspire to insecure jobs.[114] The papers presented at the seminars organised by the journal *Marxist Today* in 1988 and 1989 would be published by Stuart Hall and Martin Jacques in *New Times: The Changing Face of Politics in the 1990s.*[115] In this book, Hall points to new 'postindustrial', and 'postmodern' times, and especially 'the return of the subject', to a social, political and cultural tipping point in an economy henceforth dominated by multinationals and international financial markets in which the collective disappears and individualism prevails. What are the characteristics of post-Fordism? On the one hand, the replacement of traditional industry by new technologies, and the arrival of a decentralised and flexible form of work, accompanied by the decline of the British economy.[116] Stuart Hall also identifies it with the decline of the proletariat, the 'skilled, male, manual working-class',[117] and the subsequent development of white-collar jobs and the service society, the increasing number of part-time jobs, the 'feminisation' and 'ethnicisation' of the work force, as well as the emergence of new

[114] André Gorz, *Farewell to the Working Class: An Essay on Post-Industrial Socialism,* London, Pluto Press, 1982, p. 3.
[115] Stuart Hall and Martin Jacques, *New Times, The Changing Face of Politics in the 1990s,* London, Lawrence & Wishart, 1989.
[116] Ibid, p.118.
[117] Ibid.

kinds of social fragmentation. Stuart Hall observes the contradictions between the values of socialism and the various brands of post-Fordism, and worries about what socialism will become in the 21st century: 'Can a socialism of the 21st century revive, or even survive, which is wholly cut off from the landscapes of popular pleasures, however contradictory and 'commodified' a terrain they represent?'[118]

In this framework, postmodernism can be read as cultural change which entails a rejection of 'high modernism', the international style and the institutionalisation of the avant-gardes, turning instead toward a popular art that is integrated into daily life. It supposes a disillusion with cosmopolitism and a debate on internationalism. For Araeen, this passage takes on the form of his engagement to subject-based identity politics, with *Paki Bastard (Portrait of the Artist as a Black Person),* which is often presented as a break in his practice, which moved towards 'conceptualism'. This term was proposed by the artist Luis Camnitzer in the exhibition *Global Conceptualism: Points of Origin, 1950s-1980s,*[119] held at the Queens Museum of Art in New York in 1999, to designate the shift in art away from the production of objects towards an emphasis on the production of concepts, based on the geopolitical transformations of interest to artists such as the development of the 'Third World' and the phases of massive decolonisation between 1950 and 1973, the student uprising of 1968 (in Japan, Western Europe, Mexico, Poland, Czechoslovakia and Yugoslavia) up to the crisis of 1973 and the consequences throughout the world of the end of the cold war.

The art critic Guy Brett has highlighted how the first period of minimalist and kinetic sculptures by Rasheed Araeen, developed in his studio at St Katherine Dock, came to an end in 1971 after his reading of Frantz Fanon's *The Wretched of the Earth.* Affected by the racism underlying the murder of the British-Nigerian David Oluwale by the police near Leeds in 1969, Araeen would create the installation *For Oluwale,*

[118] Ibid.
[119] Luis Camnitzer, Jane Farver and Rachel Weiss, *Global Conceptualism,* op. cit., preface.

(1971-1973). He also joined the Black Workers movement and the collective Artists for Democracy.

He was also associated with the generation of artists gravitating around the cosmopolitism of *Signals.* In the mid-1960s, the dominance of pop art and abstract art had left little room for other artistic propositions, even if the artists who travelled between Latin America, France, the United Kingdom and the countries of the Commonwealth had intensified the cultural transfers between these areas. Gallery One run by Victor Musgrave (1953-1963) had presented artists from France, Switzerland, India, and Pakistan such as Ben Vautier and Yves Klein, Daniel Spoerri, Bridget Riley, as well as Francis Newton Souza and Avinash Chandra who were living in Great Britain. The New Vision Centre, which was directed by the South African artist Denis Bowen and Kennett Coutts-Smith, presented works by artists from the Commonwealth countries including Ahmed Parvez, Anwar Jalal Shemza and Balraj Khanna.

David Medalla, Paul Keeler, Gustave Metzger and Guy Brett were the founders of a collective and an art space called *Signals,* as well as the interdisciplinary journal of the same name, which showcased neoconcrete poetry, architecture, science, philosophy and sculpture (1964-1966). It was a research laboratory with the will to foster exchange and exhibit the works of international artists such as Lygia Clark, Sergio de Camargo, Alejandro Otero, Takis, Jesus Raphael Soto, Takis, Helio Oiticica and Li Yuan Chia.[120] Guy Brett describes *Signals* as a 'cosmopolitan, experimental and Interdisciplinary' place,[121] a definition that was fitting for a number of artist collectives that developed in the 1970s, no longer around kinetic art, but which featured participative events such as performances and happenings. In addition, at Susan Hiller's Dream Seminar, artists using different practices would meet, including the likes of Carlyle Reedy, Rasheed Araeen, Yoko Ono and Li

[120] The exhibition *Sounding Two* (1965) brought together works by Mondrian, Malevich, Duchamp, Ray, Kandinsky, Rodchenko, Klee, Schwitters, Moore, Calder, Moholy-Nagy and Naum Gabo. *Signals* became a meeting place for those involved in the international avant-garde.
[121] Guy Brett, *Exploding Galaxies, The Art of David Medalla*, London, *Third Text*, 1995, p. 50.

Yuan Chia. Then with *Artists for Democracy,* an organisation established by David Medalla in 1974, the collective experience and the cosmopolitism he wished to promote would be inscribed within a project for an art of change in line with the New Left's socialist project and providing material and cultural support for liberation movements throughout the world.

At the end of the 1970s, the term 'cosmopolitism', associated with chosen, transnational migration, was confronted with 'internationalism', which according to Kobena Mercer in *Cosmopolitan Modernism,*[122] insists on the solidarity between social classes. As the hostility towards immigrants increased, many artists left Great Britain; some moving to the United States like Frank Bowling, others travelling, like David Medalla. Whether they proposed universal abstract or conceptual art, the cosmopolitan 'Commonwealth' artists were no longer really supported by the British government. In 1978, in the framework of the State of British Art conference, Rasheed Araeen gave a talk entitled International Art, Eurocentrism, Racism, Domination.[123] It was a violent critique of the call for international art, which he defined as a kind of naive idealism hiding behind a call to European forces and to their messianic nature, considered to be the agents of international cultural domination, and in which international art would be central to a process of cultural neocolonialism. He thus highlighted the paradoxical nature of the expression 'international art', which is close to that of 'global art' used in the 2000s. Internationalism is a political term that emerged within revolutionary workers organisations. It first appeared in Great Britain around 1850, then was widely brandished during the Paris Commune (1870-1871) and used in the art world as a means to unite avant-garde artists against nationalist discourses. Araeen pointed out the porousness and friction between cosmopolitan modernism and an internationalism based on anti-imperialism and postcolonialism. He

[122] Kobena Mercer, "Introduction", in *Cosmopolitan Modernisms,* London, Iniva, MIT, 2005, p.6-23.
[123] Rasheed Araeen, «International Art, Eurocentrism Racism Domination», op. cit.

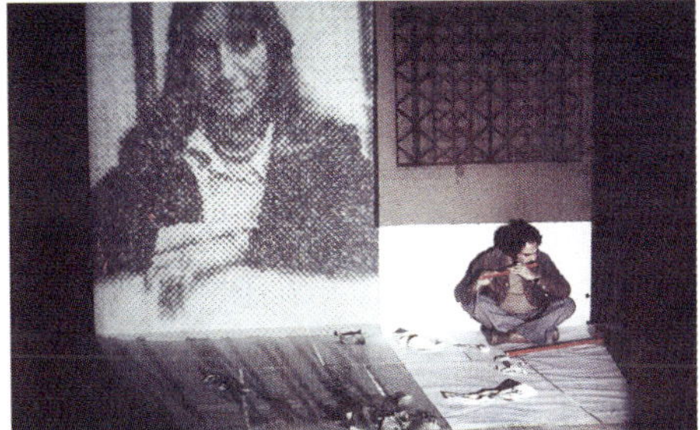

Fig.11 Rasheed Araeen, *Paki Bastard, the Artist as A Black Person*, Performance, 1977.

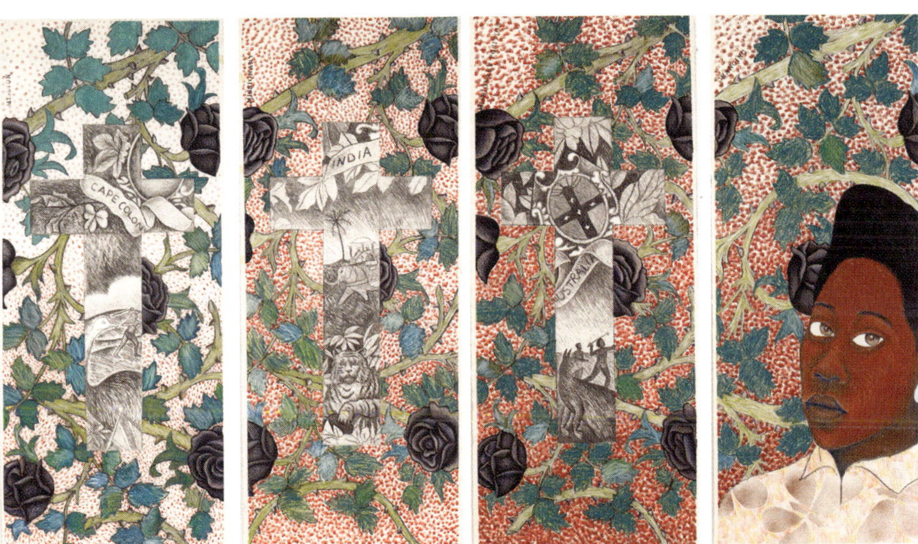

Fig.12 Sonia Boyce, *Lay Back Keep Quiet and Think of What Made Britain So Great*, Charcoal, pastel, and watercolor, 152, 5 x 65 cm, 1986.
Arts Council Collection, Southbank Centre, London © Sonia Boyce. All Rights Reserved, DACS.

would maintain this position in the editorial policy of his journals *Black Phoenix,* founded in 1978 (Fig.7), and *Third Text*, founded in 1987. The latter would be a space for discussion that highlighted the gap between artistic internationalism and cultural colonialism in the work of the foreign artists living in Great Britain. At that time, identity-based politics focusing on class, ethnicity and gender were starting to dominate critical discourse. Araeen was starting to examine his affiliations through the figure of the black-artist or "black intellectual",[124] as in *Paki Bastard, The Artist as A Black Person* (Fig.11), which evokes both an ethnic insult and the figure of the artist in the image. Araeen is one of the first artists in Great Britain who established a connection between the forms of artistic production of immigrant artists and the conditions of production and reception of artworks in the specifically British context.

When he performed *Paki Bastard* in 1977, Araeen projected some fifty slides on his gagged and hidden face; notably, some of his minimalist works, thus making the representation of the subject a core concern in his productions. His passage from kinetic and minimalistic art to performance can also be perceived in the work announcing this move. In *Making Myself Visible*, the photograph *Jheel Park, Karachi, 1974* is accompanied by a note:

> One of the important factors within this composition which obsessed man is the expression of MOVEMENT through the creation of tension between RELATIONS of different elements or objects, and this was achieved by reducing the different elements/ objects to INEQUALITY and placing them at UNEQUAL distances/ levels. Perhaps this approach unconsciously expressed the inequalities between different members of society.[125]

Meanwhile, from *Jheel Park* to *Paki Bastard*, his universalist kinetic approach mutated into an anticolonial approach, which is situated on the artist himself, in Great Britain. *Jheel Park* consisted in

[124] Ambalavaner Sivanandan, "The Liberation of Black Intellectual", in *Race and Class,* (vol.18), 1977, p. 329-343.
[125] Rasheed Araeen, Karachi, April 11, 1974, *Making Myself Visible*, op. cit, p. 64.

throwing flat white round disks on natural liquid surfaces, probably inspired by his close relationship with Li Yuan Chia. However, in 1974, he introduced power struggles and his analysis of inequalities as the result not of natural forces, but of specific social and political conditions. We can also note the importance of the documentation of the performances *Chakras* (1969-1970) and *Touch* (1970) as the inscription of the artist's body and gestures in the public space. The passage from the art of movement to the art of deconstruction was achieved through performance, but also the return of the subject, and of the author; taking distance from the semiotics of Roland Barthes, and turning to what Alain Touraine calls the 'return of the actor'.[126]

PORTRAITS OF ARTISTS AS BLACK PEOPLE

By placing the body of the artist at the centre of internationalist production, Rasheed Araeen does not refute the history of modern art, rather he questions the untenable Eurocentric philosophical project of modernity. His performing body introduces or literally produces the tension in as well as the silencing of the figure of the black artist in relation to Western art history. The gagged body, as a place of enunciation, provides viewers with a tool with which they can read the minimalist works projected on it, and which calls for a special relationship with the viewers or evokes a situation in which viewers are included in the (co-)construction of the work. Performed in the Artists for Democracy cultural centre, *Paki Bastard* brought together people involved in the art world who were contributing to the formation of collective representations. The complex relations between the place of enunciation and reception, as well as the exhibition space, art criticism, and the artist are offered up to the viewer. The space created embodies an issue (i.e., power struggles), and is also a sign of the failure of the cosmopolitan modernist project.

[126] Alain Touraine, "Le Retour de l'acteur", *Cahiers Internationaux de Sociologie,* Nouvelle série, Vol. 71, July-December 1981, p. 243-255.

Contrary to his distant and impersonal practices of kinetic art, Araeen was now constructing his discourse around the historically situated artist. This strategy is similar to what characterised the performances and photographs of Ana Mendieta, and the feminist artists living in Great Britain.

Other works often present a face at an angle, chin down, sometimes in a drawing as in *Ethnic Drawings* (1982), four 77.5 × 52.5 cm panels, or in *How Could One Paint a Self-Portrait!*, (1978-1979) (Fig.3), in which the same portrait is rendered in paint. In each of them, words are superimposed on faces, in the form of insults or stereotypes. The overloaded image is created through cluttering and polluting the clear, rational space within the frame. Araeen also describes it as a parasite of minimalism in his works made up of 9 panels:

> First, I make a rectangular minimalist space or panel, often painted green (an allusion to, for example, nature/raw/ young/ immature–all these words are taken from the English dictionary), which is cut vertically and horizontally, and then I move the four panels apart forming an empty space or cruciform.[127]

This critique of clean-cut minimalism is accompanied by his new use of figurative representations in the form of self-portraits.

In these works, Araeen highlights the figure of the artist as a political place of enunciation. Likewise from 1975 to 1989, the figures of the migrant artist and the rioter would be developed. Donald Rodney proposed *Self-Portrait: Policing the Black Community, Death in the City: Mr Winston Rose, Mr Stephen Bogle, and Mr Clinton McCurbin – A Postmodern Postmortem,* (1988). In this work, he reuses the photograph of an arrest, which was published in the journal *Ten 8,* in 1982.[128] This wilful identification with rioters appears in certain photographs of the miners' strike created in 1984 by the collective Amber, working in

[127] Rasheed Araeen, "The Artist as a post-colonial subject and this individual's journey towards the centre", op. cit., p. 249.
[128] *Ten 8,* Restricted Practices, n°7/8, 1982, John Sturrocks and Mike Abrahams, *Arrest During Disturbance in The Acre Lane, at the End of the Week of Riots Around The Country.*

Newcastle-Upon-Tyne, particularly those of Keith Pattison, in the series *Easington: August 1984*, which documents the clashes between the police and miners in County Durham. Self-portrait would truly dominate the practices of many artists in the British Black Art movement, including Chila Kumari Burman. Her series entitled *Self-Portrait* (including *This is not Me*,1992) (Fig.4) makes use of screenprint compositions with a close-up of her face, spray-painted inscriptions and Shotokan stances (particularly in 1993). The posture depicted is no longer a closed face with closed eyelids, rather it is a dynamic and proud self-affirmation. Keith Piper was working on religious and sports icons. For example, whilst the magazine *Esquire* published a cover photo explicitly expressing a link between the two, with the title 'The Passion of Mohammed Ali', Keith Piper would develop the figure of 'the lynched or crucified male body'[129] – as in *Reactionary Suicide..* He would also create figures of athletes as saints, as in *Transgressive Acts* (1993), two full-length portraits of a saint (Mohammed Ali) and a sinner (Mike Tyson). Kobena Mercer interprets this image as a reinterpretation of St. Sebastian by Mantegna (1480). Beyond the figures, the extremely regular use of rigid structures in wood or cardboard, and especially the very elongated format of the portraits also indicate a practice that is close to Italian icon paintings. Keith Piper added: 'I am interested in it and in the use of visual images of god, the use of the image to reinforce ideological messages. The catholic religion took that from earlier version of cultures, with god spirits as visual things.'[130]

In his 1982 *Reactionary Suicide: Black Boys Keep Swinging (or Another Nigger Died Today)* (Fig.14), Keith Piper interprets David Hammons' painting *Injustice Case* (1970), in which the US flag is almost totally hidden by the negative print of a man tied up and gagged on a chair. This work is in direct reference to Bobby Seale, the co-founder of the Black Panthers, who had been tied up during the trial of the Chicago Seven.[131]

[129] Kobena Mercer, in *Keith Piper, Relocating the Remains,* London, Iniva, 1999, p. 59.
[130] My interview with Keith Piper in Islington, 22 April 2015, op. cit..
[131] Bobby Seale was an American civil rights activist and a leader in the Black Panthers movement. He co-founded the Black Panther Party for Self Defense in 1966. The Chicago Seven were seven defendants accused of inciting to revolt during the protests at the 1968 Democratic National Convention. Seale was the eighth defendant initially charged in this affair.

This 'body-print' illustrates the injustice in the treatment of prisoners from minority groups in the United States. In *Reactionary Suicide*, the man is also forced into submission and judged at the centre of a painting in the colours of the flag. The tie that strangles its protagonist reminds us of the lynchings and hangings in the United States perpetuated by the Ku Klux Klan. However, the design of his T-shirt is reminiscent of the punk period and resituates the work in the England of the 1970s. Keith Piper makes his character's red basketball shoes break out of the frame; in this way, going beyond the canvas and a simply political interpretation of his work.

The reintegration of the figure, worked on by feminist artists in particular, was a stumbling block. Often considered to be a political space in which gender and the experience of the subject can be represented, it is also a place for questioning art history. Rasheed Araeen, as Adrian Piper and Mona Hatoum, use the figuration of the artist as a disruptive element, and therefore one that reflects upon the universalist discourse of modernity.

CONCEPTUAL SHIFTS AND DECONSTRUCTIONS TACTICS FROM 1980S TO 1990S: SONIA BOYCE VERSUS SARAH LUCAS.

In the 1980s, the productions of Sonia Boyce, as well as those of Black feminist artists took distance from the essentialist framework in which the works of the Blk Art Group and British Black Art emerged. By developing an artistic position that was a place for deconstructing and questioning the dominant artistic models, Sonia Boyce shifted the problematic of *'race, class and gender'* toward subaltern studies and feminist studies. In the 1990s, Sonia Boyce's works put into play critical tools she shares with Young British Artists, the generation of artists linked to Goldsmiths Art College, which included Sarah Lucas.[132]

[132] Thus, *Along the Lines of Resistance*, an exhibition organised by Sutapa Biswas, Sarah Edge and Claire Slattery in 1988, displayed works by the Northern Irish artist Anne Tallentire, as well as the drawings of Lesley Sanderson, the installations of Marlene Smith, the photographs of Sonia Boyce *(Loving in a Cold Climate)*, *Measure of Distance* by Mona Hatoum (1988), and an installation on racism and institutional sexism by Lubaina Himid and Maud Sulter (*Gold Blooded Warrior*, 1988). The catalogue includes a text by Prathiba Parmar.

The staging of a self-portrait within British imperialist history can be observed in *Lay Back, Keep Quiet and Think of What Made Britain So Great* by Sonia Boyce (1986). Three vertically-placed rectangular panels display three conquered territories – the south of Africa, India and Australia – symbolised in the form of a Christian cross. A fourth panel offers us a self-portrait of the artist. The flower motif covering the four canvases is evocative of William Morris' Arts and Crafts work. The 'red' rose is the so-called 'Tudor rose', the rose of the British monarchy. This flower, which is now significantly black, appears on each of the stems, and evokes the cultural ambivalence of the nation. In the upper left corner of the four pastels are engraved the inscriptions in capital letters: 'Mission', 'Missionary', and 'Missionary position', then her self-portrait, *Changing*. Sonia Boyce plays on the relations between religion, colonisers and the colonised. The cross symbolises both conquest and the 'civilising mission', and erases the subject and its identity. The affirmation of identity and the growing awareness of the visibility of the black subject were enabling a 'change' in representation. Gayatri C. Spivak published *Can the Subaltern Speak* in 1988, a text that denounces the supposed neutrality of the Western subject for the theoreticians of deconstruction Michel Foucault, Gilles Deleuze and Jacques Derrida. Gayatri C. Spivak proposes a reflexive critique of the ideology at work in the position of the subject within the State and the political economy. She denounces the patriarchal reading of Marx:

> The relationship between global capitalism (exploitation in economics) and nation-state alliances (domination in geopolitics is so macrological that it cannot account for the micrological texture of power. To move toward such an accounting one must move toward theories of ideology –of subject formations that micrologically and often erratically operate the interests that congeal the macrologies.[133]

[133] Gayatri Chakravorty Spivak, "Can the Subaltern Speak" (1988), Rosalind Morris (ed.), *Can the Subaltern Speak? Reflections on the History of an Idea,* New York, Columbia University Press, p. 247.

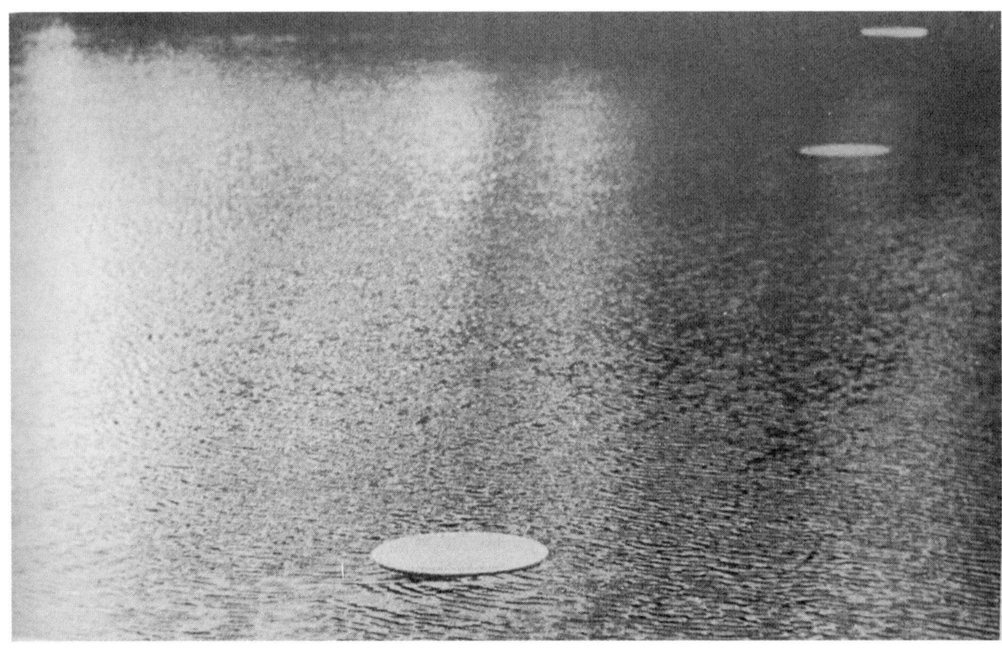

Fig.13 Rasheed Araeen, *Jheel Park,*
Performance,1974.

At the heart of this project is the proposition to examine the representational possibilities for subjects (particularly women) who are deprived of a 'voice' and visibility, based on a rereading of the subaltern classes proposed by Antonio Gramsci. These different heritages push the artists to activate the dynamics of feminist art, according to which 'the personal is political', while articulating a local space (London, British) and a global space (the general history of imperialism). Sonia Boyce uses the portrait to create the figure of the artist-witness, situated in the British postcolonial context, and more exactly in the metropolis within the Commonwealth.

Boyce, like Lubaina Himid,[134] worked on drawing and painting from 1982 to 1989, thereby distancing herself from the practices of installation and performance central to the work of the American feminist artists living in London at that time, which included Susan Hiller and Mary Kelly. Boyce proposed an equation between the codes of Englishness, and its symbols and elements in the cultural history of Great Britain, which she associated with the representation of a personal narrative. At this time, she was working with pastels and drawing in a realist manner. She was also working on 'magical realism',[135] drawing on the decorative scenery of Frida Khalo, which can be compared to Douanier Rousseau, as well as the primitivism of Paula Modersohn-Becker. It was her response to the feminist productions that were producing gendered international conceptual art. In 1974, a collective known as the Blackwomen's Creativity Project was formed. The portrait artist Maud Sulter was then one of the writers in the feminist publishing collective Sheba. In 1990, she published *Passion: Discourses on Blackwomen's Creativity,*[136] a survey of 'black' feminist artistic practices, made by Ingrid Pollard and Sulter, just after the First National Black Art Convention. Pollard, a photographer, was publishing in the feminist magazines *Spare Rib*

[134] As well as Maud Sulter, Lesley Sanderson and Sutapa Biswas.
[135] Franz Roh, *Postexpressionnisme — Réalisme magique — Problèmes de la peinture européenne la plus récente,* (1925), Dijon, Les Presses du réel, 2013.
[136] Maud Sulter (ed.), *Passion: Discourses on Blackwomen's Creativity,* UFP, Hebden Bridge, 1990.

and *OutWrite*. Together, they documented the literary and artistic works of Sonia Boyce, Chila Kumari Burman, Lubaina Himid, Maud Sulter, Claudette Johnson, and Sutapa Biswas, as well as of the Asian Women Writer's Collective.[137] Black feminist critical thought was drawing on sources in cultural studies and black cultural studies.[138] In his article "White Women Listen!", Hazel Carby critiques feminist theories for their indifference to the situation of black women, and declares that 'Both white feminist theory and practice have to recognize that white women stand in a power relation as oppressors of black women.'[139] This British black feminism[140] was also constructed within activist groups that emerged in the 1970s. Very focused on the issues of exclusion and the various representations of the British identity, the British feminists created the OWAAD (Organisation for Women of Asian and African Descent) in 1978, then Southall Black Sisters, as well as Women Against Fundamentalism. This feminism was therefore inscribed within a revolutionary artistic internationalism that was against formalist abstraction.

As of the 1990s and the end of identity-based politics, the demands from the government were no longer for equality, but for

[137] The artists Maud Sulter and Lubaina Himid were the directors of the Elbow Room gallery.

[138] In Great-Britain, the major disseminators of postcolonial critical thought and the works of Black artists were the journals *Third Text*, directed by Rasheed Araeen as of 1987, and *Ten 8*, which was more oriented toward the visual arts and founded by three photographers from Birmingham: Derek Bishton, Brian Homer and John Reardon. Its first issue appeared in 1979. Whilst *Third Text* was above all a platform for reflection, featuring debates on art criticism between Rasheed Araeen, Eddie Chambers, Gilane Tawadros and Kobena Mercer, as well as Stuart Hall and Paul Gilroy, *Ten 8*'s model was the photography journal *Camerawork*, and it showcased the image itself.

[139] Hazel V. Carby, "White Women Listen! Black Feminism and the Boundaries of Sisterhood", in Houston A. Baker, *Black British Cultural Studies*, op. cit, p. 63. Black feminists as well as black feminist artists rapidly set themselves apart from white feminist movements.

[140] This orientation is supported by Heidi Safia Mirza, who in the collective work *Black British Feminism* assesses the history of the discipline through illustrations of the different aspects of feminism, from the history of migrations and lesbian identities to the representation of the body and the formation of a third wave of feminism. The way these artists put the past into perspective, and the references to Western art history in their works link private space and public space. These different artists were to a large extent trained at the University of Leeds, a hotbed of radical thought (Griselda Pollock, Terry Atkinson, Fred Orton, and John Tagg taught there), or followed the example of the American artist Mary Kelly and the feminist thought of London. See Heidi Safia Mirza (ed.), *Black British Feminism: A Reader*, London; New York, Routledge, 1997.

difference and diversity. The politics taking into consideration and promoting the representations of Afro-Caribbean and Asian communities came to an end, coinciding with the only major panoramic exhibition of British Black Art, *The Other Story,* organised by Rasheed Araeen at the Hayward Gallery in 1989. After this shift of 1989,[141] Sonia Boyce adopted a conceptual artistic vocabulary and took distance from the politics of representation. She no longer used the self-portrait as a place of enunciation for gendered and race issues. She abandoned collage, drawing and painting and started doing performances using video and installations of her thoughts on a depersonalised and socially constructed body. Her first such works were developed just after *The Other Story* where her pastels were exhibited, while Sonia Boyce soon after started collecting bags of frizzy hair and working with this material.

With other artists, such as Tracey Emin and Sarah Lucas, she debated gender politics and the ethnic-based approach. The identity-based politics of gender and blackness were indeed very central to the practices of this generation of artists associated with the class of 1988 at Goldmsiths College called the 'Young British Artists'. This generation developed according to an entrepreneurial logic, which was most remarkably embodied in the relationship linking Damien Hirst and the advertising executive Charles Saatchi. Since the election of Margaret Thatcher, the British welfare state, socialism and Marxism had collapsed,[142] the unions had lost power, the tensions between minority groups had intensified and regionalisms had developed. The deconcentration of power toward the regions had been the subject of debate since 1979, whilst the nationalist parties such as the Scottish National Party and Plaid Cymru in Wales were getting stronger and stronger. IRA bombs touched Harrods and the City. In 1993, a first cease-fire was proclaimed in Ireland, but in 1996, part of Canary Wharf was destroyed by an IRA bomb. That same year, US troops

---

[141] Sophie Orlando, "Sonia Boyce: Post- 1989 Art Strategies", *Critique d'art,* n°43, 2014, p.110-125.
[142] The CPGB (Communist Party of Great Britain) became the Democratic Left in 1991.

invaded Iraq with support from Great Britain. As a result, the debates on cultural identity were particularly intense and related to a new definition of Britishness, characterised by Linda Colley as the feeling of belonging to a common culture based on monarchy, Protestantism, democracy and empire,[143] or by J.G.A Pocock in terms of the wide range of trans-Atlantic trade and transfer.[144] The provocations, transfigurations, irony and anti-intellectual stance of the Young British Artists were interpreted as forms of treason and a renouncement of any commitment by artists to a social project. Yet at the same time, they were very warmly welcomed by the British intelligentsia, which was seeking a new icon representative of British art on the international scene that could rival with American art, which had been sovereign in the academic world and art market in Great Britain since the Second World War. Whilst the Thatcher years imposed the return of Victorian values and 'Englishness' in the world of culture, the 1990s would be placed under the sign of multicultural Britishness with the overhaul of the Labour Party under Tony Blair.[145]

Sarah Lucas and Sonia Boyce have some common references; however, the places from which they speak are different, enabling us to identify their distinct tactics. These artists drew on the gendered body, particularly as of the mid-1990s, which was perceived as a space in which the politics of sexuality and gender could be discussed. Their politics of the body construct different place of utterance, through the recurrent use of an object: panty hose. Sarah Lucas mixes media in the installation *Self-Portraits and More Sex Woman In A Tub,* 2000 (Fig.15), in which there is a coat hanger suspended in a bathtub from which hang two fried eggs and beige nylon panty hose. She associates an intimate space that is common to everyone (the bathtub), a caricatured construct that represents the female body (fried eggs), and a piece of women's clothing (panty

[143] Linda Colley, *Forging the Nation (1707-1837),* (1992), New Heaven, Yale University Press, 2009.
[144] J.G.A Pocock, Speech at the New Zealand Historical Association, 1973.
[145] See *Ambitions for Britain, Labour's Manifesto 2001* (available at Labour.org.uk) and Chris Smith (ed.), *A New Cultural Framework,* London, DCMS, 1997.

Fig.14 Keith Piper, *Reactionary Suicide: Black Boys Keep Swinging (or Another Nigger Died Today,*1
Acrylic and mixed media on canvas, 182,88 x 121,9

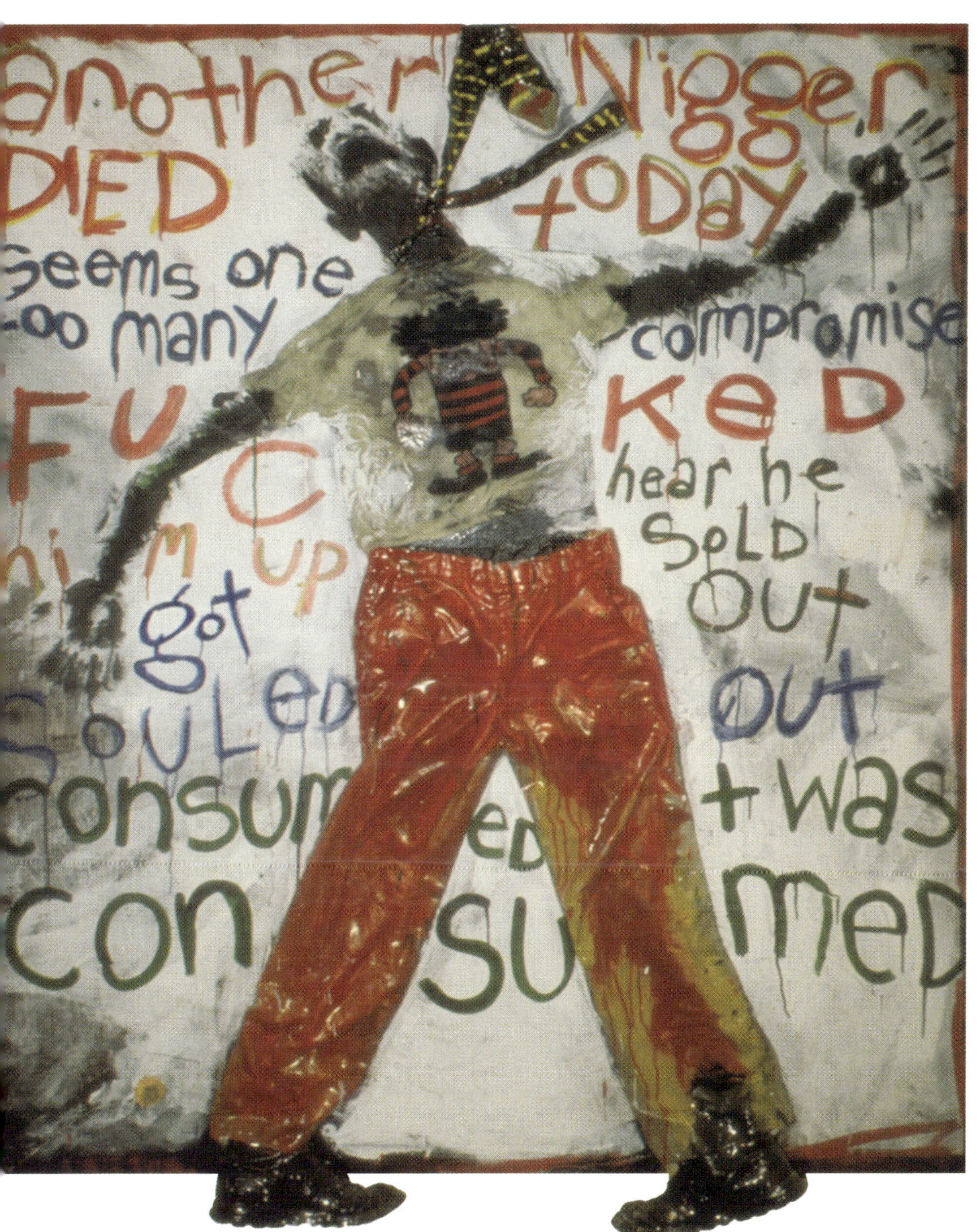
another Nigger
DIED
Seems one
too many
FU   KED
C
M UP
got
SOULED
consumed
compromise
hear he
sold
OUT
OUT
+ was
con   su   med
today

hose). The fried eggs are a referential tool, used in a metonymic process, whilst the panty hose constitute an index immediately belonging to the feminine world, or even defining femininity itself. Panty hose are widely used in her series *Bunny,* stuffed toy rabbits, with their legs spread apart mime both the icon of *Playboy,* the American erotic magazine, and the inflatable doll. The panty hose are a tool for making a pair of legs. Stuffed with pink, flesh-coloured or black cotton, they are often affixed to a chair and the back of the chair mimes the hips and the bust to which are attached long arms or big ears. *Bunny* is an installation or a photograph, which enacts a 'trashy' style, a situation in which the female body is offered up to us, and sometimes even fastened by clamps (*Bunny Gets Snookered,* 1997). The look of the 'dolls' is similar to the studies of postures staged in the self-portraits of Lucas, which play on the masculine codes of the working classes. The *Bunny* series depicts the representations of a socially situated body, but with no face, therefore a representation of a relationship of authority in the constitution of gender and in the representations of sexuality.

In Boyce's *Three Legs Stuffed with Hair* (1995), the close-up view obliges the viewer to enter into close contact with the subject, even into its intimacy because of the tiny holes in the panty hose from which the curly black hair emerges. Three completely impersonal photographs designate three parts of the body that cannot be linked to any specific face. The folds in the panty hose generate the erotic body.[146] Should the three photographs be read as a narration from left to right? Obliterating any external context, the first photograph presents a very close-in sidelong shot of the hair, principal motif on which the photographer focuses. The tip of the panty hose, in the foreground, occupies the left third of the photograph (skin, breast, private parts?), whilst the curve of the panty hose, which disappears

[146] Hans Bellmer, *Petite anatomie de l'image*, Paris, Allia, 2010.

into the background to the right, does not designate any specific part of the body. The second photograph is a frontal view of the stitching of the panty hose, both a sign of how it was made and a designation of the direction in which to read the image, as well as a link between the two other images. It delineates an undefined flat form. The last photograph presents a thick panty hose, filled with afro braids. The framing designates a sculpture, a cylinder within which there is soft, silky tissue, with no hair. The stitches are from this point of view three ornaments. The sculpture is thus the transformation of the body, which has become an orifice. Sonia Boyce designates the relationship between the representation of afro hair and desire, as Mary Ann Doane and Rosemary Betterton have analysed it in psychoanalytical terms,[147] as the place of desire and a foil. In these three pictures, Boyce proposes a narrative on the construction of how we look at hair as a sign of belonging to a gender and to an ethnic group, particularly through the three steps in the framing, which, like John Berger's *Ways of Seeing,*[148] indicates the circumstances of reception of an image.

Hair is also a cultural and social marker, which shapes issues related to race, gender, beauty and sexuality and the stereotypes associated with them. The politicization of frizzi hairdos took on importance in the United States in the 1960s, and increasingly embodied the pride of belonging to the Black culture. These hairdos are also cultural heritage as seen in the photographs of Marsha Hunt by Horace Ové. Hunt, who was a singer in the musical comedy *Hair,* also appeared nude on the cover of *Vogue*, in a photograph taken by Patrick Lichfield in 1969. There are also the portraits of Angela Davis, the American Communist activist, taken by Gavin Jantjes at the beginning of the 1970s. Furthermore, hair is literally the sign of the

[147] Rosemary Betterton, *Intimate Distance, Women, Artists and the Body,* London, New York, Routledge, 1996. Mary Ann Doane, *Femmes Fatales, Feminism, Film Theory, Psychoanalysis,* London, Routledge, 1991.
[148] John Berger, *Ways of Seeing,* London, Penguin, 1972.

body or the part taken for the whole.[149] The suggestion that the hair belongs to a specific body breaks with the process of desingularisation and generalisation of cultural identities enacted by the framing. Who is speaking and to whom? Is Sonia Boyce's work here closer to Tracey Emin's *My Bed* than to Sarah Lucas' *Bunny*? In *My Bed* (1998), Tracey Emin comments upon the representation of the woman in classical and modern painting (as an odalisque or an 'Olympiad'). The bed is the bedroom, the intimate, the space in which the objects of her daily life pile up—her slippers, cigarettes, dirty clothes and knickers, bath towels, panty hose, newspapers, condoms, and closed suitcases. The artist makes the bed look as real as possible with an air of autofiction placing her stained knickers among the rest of the mess, the traces of a life of drinking (bottles), tears (handkerchiefs), distress (wrinkled sheets), and panty hose left behind on a bed. Tracey Emin's work is based on a fundamental principle of equivalence between the artist's studio, her bed and intimacy, which are often placed in separate spheres in the pictorial regime to make a distinction between the viewer, the artist and the model—object of (her) desire—and not the artist's sexuality. *My Bed* unveils the artist's intimacy, which is in direct contact with the gaze of the viewer. In a very different way, *Three Legs Stuffed with Hair* establishes the very conditions of representation of a masculine gaze, as well as the tools with which representation itself is constructed. She accomplishes this by the ways in which she frames her compositions, the sequence of which constructs a space of observation. The three photographs (by means of a narrative linking the three compositions) provide the viewer with the tools for deconstructing her objects (hair, panty hose). The hair is an extension,

[149] The panty hose opens the way for a more in-depth exploration of the theme of the body, skin and the subject for Mona Hatoum who uses her hair (an index of the body) to make balls she scatters on the floor in Recollection, 1995. She would also use her hair to weave the patterns of the Palestinian keffieh, alluding in these works to the artistic feminism of the 1970s, expressed in the slogan 'the personal is political' (Mona Hatoum, Keffieh, 1993-1999).

not of the artist's body, but of the black female body. This black female body designates and defuses the erotic stereotype of the 'black continent'. In a word, the enunciative situation serves to establish the conditions of reception of the viewer, who is given simultaneously a context (the space of representation, and thoughts on how representations are constructed) and the tools for deconstructing these representations (the evocation of the erotic black body by the panty hose and the different framing). The principle of framing and the hair act therefore in the same way as the gesture of tearing up the black card in *Destruction of the National Front.* They are marked by a gesture and the trace of a physical body, and open a space for taking distance from representation. This approach must be distinguished from the icon of the represented body (Sarah Lucas) or simply from the function of an enunciative situation (Tracey Emin enacting the intimacy of the artist Tracey Emin for the benefit of the viewer). The composition and hair are the keys for reading the work and constitute the place from which is generated the possible deconstruction of representations of class, race, gender, and sex in Western art history.

My analysis shows a scission between the different works of Sarah Lucas and Sonia Boyce. While the two artists work on the re-presentation (of women's sexuality) from the point of view of the powers of the viewer and in particular gendered constructions, Sonia Boyce draws on the discursive tactics of conceptual art and proposes a two-fold, poststructuralist reading of the image. Viewers are given the context in which identity-based racial and sexual representations are elaborated as well the formal tools for deconstructing these representations. They can thus situate themselves at this intersection. Therefore, her break with Sarah Lucas is consummated by the creation of this 'active' place of enunciation, a veritable critical space specific to Sonia Boyce's artistic productions of the 1990s.

Fig.15 Sarah Lucas, *Woman In A Tub*,
Bathtub, taps, hanger, fried eggs, tights, 120 x 99 x 70 cm
installation *Self-Portraits and More Sex*, 2000.

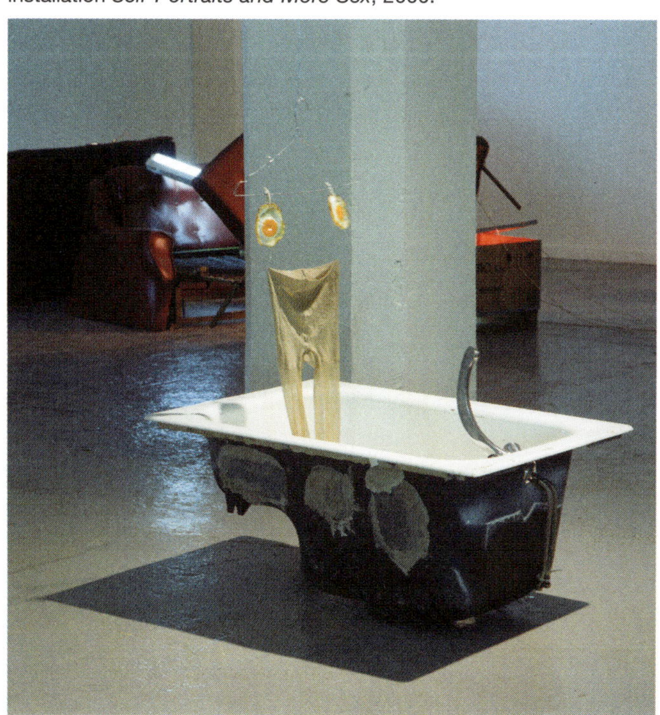

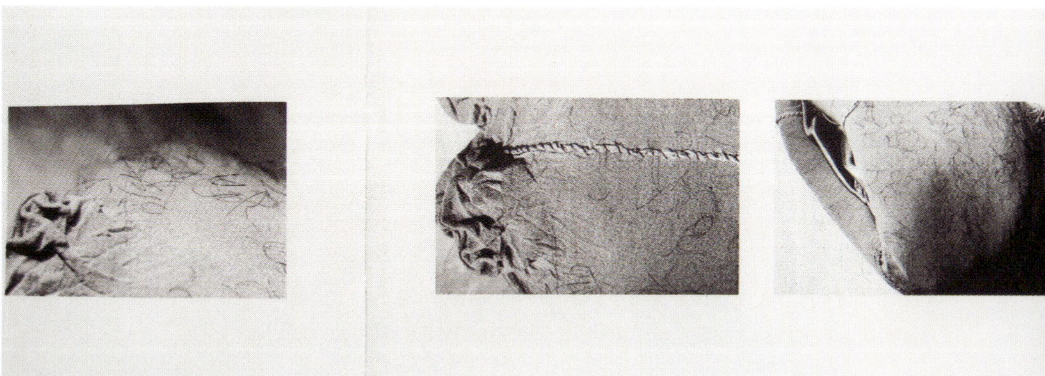

Fig.16 Sonia Boyce: *Three Legs Stuffed with Hair*,
Color photography, 1995.

THE 1990S: NEW INTERNATIONALISM — A REASSESSMENT OF UNIVERSALISM?

After the period of identity-based politics developed since the 1970s, the 1990s ushered in not only the dissemination of the political project of cultural studies, which went viral and had a major impact on other disciplines, but also a reassessed form of universalism, which was played out as a debate on 'new internationalism'.

In 1991, the Arts Council published the study *The Institute of New International Visual Arts*[150] and defined some 'emerging concepts', which included 'New Internationalism'. Confronted with a definition of art history that was limited to Europe and the United States, New Internationalism wanted to be inclusive, and proposed to place 'the achievements of the majority of cultures of the world into discourses, the exhibitions and the history of contemporary visual arts.'[151] Its response was therefore institutional.[152] The cultural politics in favour of 'diversity', which emerged in the late 1990s and early 2000s, would shape the orientations of a new art centre, the Institute of New International Visual Arts. After the failure and the closing of the galleries that supported British Black Art (the Horizon Gallery in 1991 and the Black-Art Gallery in 1992), and the disappearance of the OBAALA (Organisation for Black Art Advancement and Learning Activities), the Arts Council decided to finance a project that would assert the unity of the productions of black artists, and of their history.[153]

[150] This shift toward internationalism led to the creation of the Institute of New International Visual Arts in 1994. The Institute contributed to the dissemination of an image of cultural difference within the National Education programme and the educational services of museums. Gavin Jantjes, Eddie Chambers, and Rasheed Araeen, as well as Gilane Tawadros, Lubaina Himid and especially Sunil Gupta participated actively in the birth of the project.

[151] *The Institute of New International Visual Arts,* London, Iniva, London Arts Boards, Arts Council, 1991, p.7.

[152] Gilane Tawadros, *Changing States, Contemporary Art and Ideas in an Era of Globalisation*, London, Iniva, 2004, published on the tenth anniversary of this venue, provides an overview of the activities organised at the Iniva since its opening. Coco Fusco, Stuart Hall, Gavin Jantjes, David Medalla, and Keith Piper flirt with great talent with Zined Sedira and Hamad Butt who cohabit in turn a space that also welcomes Chris Ofili, Yinka Shonibare and Aubrey Williams.

[153] On this subject, see Richard Hylton, *The Nature of the Beast,* op.cit. The Arts Council also provided financial support for private initiatives such as the journal *Third Text,* directed by Rasheed Araeen, the Aavaa, an archive set up by Eddie Chambers, and Autograph, an association of black photographers.

The proceedings of the conference Global Visions, Towards a New Internationalism (1994),[154] edited by Jean Fisher, establish a history of the notion of internationalism going back to 1989. The French exhibition *Magicians of the World*, which became the mouthpiece of New Internationalism in 1989, is presented as the failure of the Western vision of multiculturalism. It was indeed unable to justify displaying primitive works of art alongside Western art, or Australian Aboriginal art next to abstract American expressionism. According to Rasheed Araeen,[155] decolonisation did not put an end to Western hegemony over the East. Much to the contrary, he argues that postwar internationalism is nothing more than continued domination, simply updated during the cold war with its new geopolitical rallying cry.[156]

Beyond the dissensions, New Internationalism took on the challenge of defusing the opposition between centre and periphery, turning toward an international approach that was not Eurocentric. It took action just as major exhibitions were running in Paris, *Magicians of the World* organised by Jean-Hubert Martin, and the Havana Biennial in Cuba, curated by Gerardo Mosquera. It was also the champion of postcolonial thought, which was analysed by Homi Bhabha in *The Location of Culture* as a history of postcolonial migrations.[157] Sunil

[154] Rasheed Araeen, "New Internationalism, or the Multiculturalism of Global Bantustans", in Rasheed Araeen and Jean Fisher, *Global Visions, Towards a New Internationalism in the Visual Arts*, London, Kala Press, Iniva, 1994.

[155] In *Global Visions*, Rasheed Araeen warns once again about the possible abuses of a multiculturalism, with concepts created and maintained by Western critics based on 18th century thought, which he opposes to 'Third World' postcolonial thought.

[156] Modernism and its rewriting are also central in the discussions of Nikos Papastergiadis, who interprets this process in terms of a conflict between the local and the global and the modern and the international. Nikos Papastergiadis, *The Complicity of Culture: Hybridity and New Internationalism*, Manchester, Cornerhouse, n°4, 1994, p. 49, '*At the beginning of the century European artists stretched the boundaries of modernism as they incorporated and experimented with non-European art forms. As the century comes to a close we observe a different level of fascination. The focus has moved from the artefact to the art practice. From the static object to the marginalized strategies of the colonized of the diasporized. There is now a heightened consciousness of borders and limits and art production seems more preoccupied with the paradoxes of content; a re-negotiation of the local and the global, rather than the determination of the "progressive" path towards the universal.*'

[157] Homi Bhabha, *The Location of Culture*, New York, London, Routledge, 1994.

Gupta, who was then at the head of the OVA (Organisation for Visual Arts), organised the exhibition *Disrupted Borders*, at the Ikon Gallery in 1994. According to Gavin Jantjes, it became a visual manifesto for the idea of internationalism.[158] In 1998, the year in which the *Sensation* exhibition was held at the Royal Academy, bringing together works from Charles Saatchi's collection, Gavin Jantjes published *A Fruitful Incoherence: Dialogues with Artists on Internationalism*, in collaboration with the Iniva and Gilane Tawadros. This book included interviews with Susan Hiller, Carlos Capelan, Marlene Dumas, Svetlana Kopystiansky, Marie Jo Lafontaine, David Medalla and Huang Yong Ping. Its objective was to let the artists speak for themselves, without the mediation of theory or art criticism, and to discuss terms such as 'cultural difference', 'hybridity', 'postcolonialism' and 'syncretism'. The lexicon in this publication proposes several definitions of internationalism, from Gavin Jantjes' 'a post-war phenomenon that sought an alternative to the rampant imperial nationalisms that lay at the heart of both world wars',[159] to others by writers, artists, exhibition curators, and theoreticians of postcolonial studies such as Olu Oguibe, Homi K. Bhabha, Geeta Kapur and Hou Hanru. The lexicon also provides a provisional definition of *New Internationalism*: 'A non-hegemonic project of cultural interaction which gives equal acknowledgement to the creative achievements of all people within, and in the making of, a new history of art.'[160] However, the choice of artists, which included the likes of David Medalla as an artist developing his career in Great Britain, indicates more of a return to the already existing notions of cosmopolitism and international art than a moving on to a horizon beyond them.

[158] Another event confirmed the institutional shift toward internationalism. According to Richard Hylton, the exhibition *Africa95* also marked the retreat of African art from the realm of anthropology and from the vocabulary of the 'primitive'. Linking more than ten events in various London galleries, from the Whitechapel to the Serpentine as well as the Ikon Gallery in Birmingham, the Bluecoat Gallery, and the Tate Gallery in Liverpool, not to mention the Arnolfini in Bristol, *Africa95* was first of all a response to the Royal Academy's exhibition *Africa: The Art of a Continent,* which was unable to bring together works from the contemporary period.
[159] Gavin Jantjes (ed.), *A Fruitful Incoherence: Dialogues with Artists on Internationalism*, London, Iniva, 1998, p.16.
[160] Ibid. p. 159.

In a famous article, Kobena Mercer defined a shift between the generations of the 1980s and 1990s as a dialogue between *'ethnicity and internationality'.*[161] He opposes two logics that were developing simultaneously: that of the Young British Artists (which include Tracey Emin and Sarah Lucas, as well as Chris Ofili and Yinka Shonibare), which was a kind of localism, and the new internationalism project supported by the Iniva (Gilane Tawadros, Gavin Jantjes, and Sunil Gupta), which was a form of pluralism. This tension would be dissipated in the 1990s through the process of globalisation, which on the one hand, opened up a huge space for the art market, while making the cultural policies of States disappear; and on the other hand, made the subject of cultural diversity hypervisible, with the development of mass black culture. Thus, the international exhibitions such as *Magicians of the World* (1989), *The Other Story* (1989), and *The Decade Show* (1990) are nothing more than an illustration of this compromise between internationalism and ethnicity.

In light of works by Rasheed Araeen and Sonia Boyce, several considerations help to nuance Mercer's analysis. First, the categories 'Young British Artists' and 'British Black Art' are much more porous than the ones defined by Mercer. Indeed, the Young British Artists and exponents of British Black Art never really constituted a homogeneous artistic group, either politically, aesthetically or in their artistic approaches. Whilst the artists Sonia Boyce and Sarah Lucas as well as Mona Hatoum and Tracey Emin have common references and tools, we must still analyse in detail the different uses they make of them. In addition, between the end of the 1970s and the beginning of the 1990s the political context itself had changed with the birth of postmodernism and the passage to post-Fordism, and as a result the implementation of specific tactics vis-à-vis the artistic internationalism revived in 1989.

[161] Kobena Mercer, "Ethnicity and Internationality, New British Art and Diaspora-Based Blackness", in *Third Text*, n°49, winter 1999-2000, p. 51-62.

Finally, the artistic and curatorial productions of the 1990s and 2000s proposed contradictory definitions of globalisation. On the one hand, it was considered to be a principle of cultural homogenization within a globalised economy, and on the other, at the Havana Biennial, Gerardo Mosquera conceived of it as a decentring of narratives and a rewriting of modernity, without the universalist project of the Enlightenment.

The self-portraits of Rasheed Araeen and Sonia Boyce are milestones in the practices linked to activist portrait painting between 1975 and 1989. The representation of the situated subject during this period of time enacts their rejection of cosmopolitism. Araeen broke with the cosmopolitism of kinetic art to re-explore the realm of the situated subject; whilst Boyce painted self-portraits until she realised it was a dead end and that identity politics were over. She then opted to reopen a generic place of enunciation: "Black women".

The debates on new internationalism that began in 1989 coincide with the end of British Black Art and combine with the realisation of the failure of their own narrative based on identity and the Afro-Caribbean and Asian migratory experience of the artists, played out in the travelling exhibition *The Other Story* (1989). This event marked the urgent need to dissociate the argument developed in the works vis-à-vis the history of art (in particular of modernism) with a situated social narrative of the peoples of the Commonwealth. Sonia Boyce's change in strategy and her work that comes to terms with the politics of sexuality and gender show her critical position with respect to the return of internationalism, which she perceives to be a horizon of expectation within the debates on artistic globalisation and global art. *Three Legs Stuffed With Hair* (1995) enacts the main features of her new critical approach: it enters into dialogue with the visual forms inherited from conceptual art and places in it the tools for deconstructing categories, whilst elaborating the foundations of a feminist internationalism.

CHAPTER IV. POLITICAL CULTURES OF THE BRITISH
ARTISTIC SCENES

*My analysis of specific works of British Black Art draws attention to
the need for new studies on this art. The most urgent research to conduct
concerns the links between Black feminists and performative and videography
practices in Great Britain; however, the literary and poetic aspects of these
artistic productions have also been neglected. Above all, there is a need to
study the transnational affiliations between the productions of Black Art and
above all else, its attachment to European conceptualism. This final chapter
will reflect upon the cultural affiliations between the artistic scenes in Great
Britain as of the 1990s. In particular, I will study the works of Chila Kumari
Burman as a crossroads of the different cultural and political heritages of the
New Left, then its decline and replacement by new transnational paradigms.
Whilst the critical theory emerging from cultural studies is largely associated
with Black Art, many artists developed a practice more largely inspired by the
splitting up and overhaul of British left wing parties.*

PUNK POP ROCOCO: BRITISH CULTURAL MOTIFS EMBEDDED IN THE
PRACTICES OF CHILA KUMARI BURMAN.

I would like to critique the argument concerning the supposed
anti-theoretical shift in the art of the 1990s, which is usually associated
with artists such as Tracey Emin and Sarah Lucas in Great Britain, but
can also be seen in the works of the photographers Paul Reas and Ingrid
Pollard and of the visual artist Jeremy Deller. The works of British Black
Art have created a privileged place for observing modern and

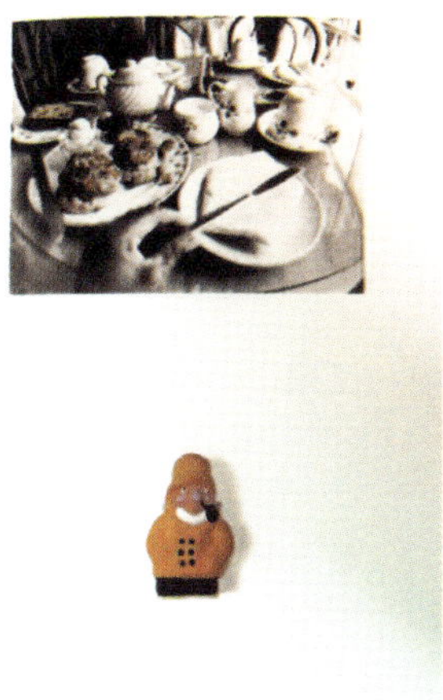

Fig.17 Ingrid Pollard, *Seaside Serie*, 1/11,
Hand-tinted silver gelatin prints
24 x 20 cm, 3d objects and texts,1989.

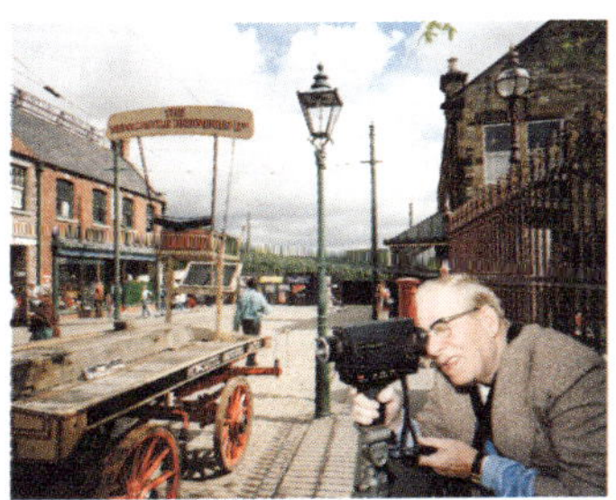

Fig.19 Paul Reas, *Flogging A Dead*
Horse Serie, *Man with a Movie Camera*,
Lightjet print 50, 8 x 60 x 96 cm
1985-1993.

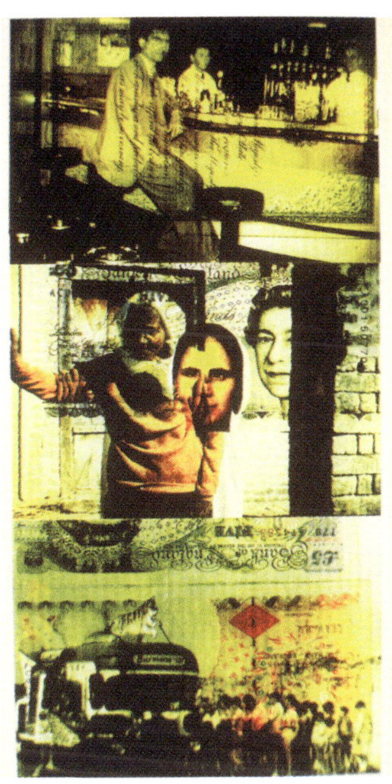

Fig.18 Chila Kumari Burman, *Dad on Ship
Arriving in Britain, My Mum and Grandmother,
The Three Queens, Ice Cream Van on Freshfiled Beach*,
Cibachrome, 58,42 x 30, 48 cm, 1995.

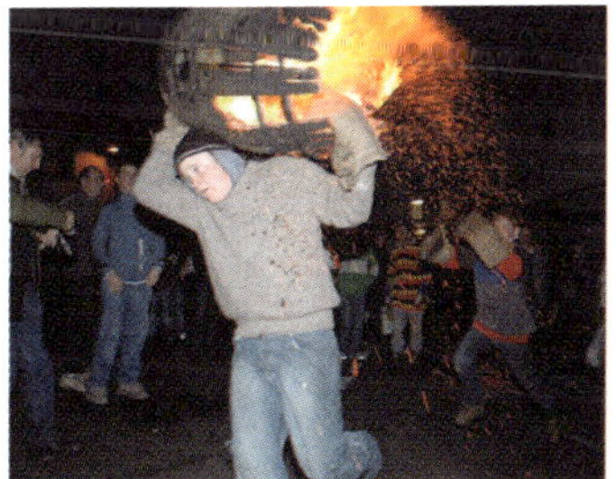

Fig.20 Jeremy Deller et Alan Kane,
Folk Archive, Tar Barrel Rolling Ottery st Mary, 2005.
(photo Jessica Mallock)

contemporary art history, which is grounded in the heritage stemming from American theories of art (Black Literature, modernist and postmodernist debates, and semiotics) and in the foundations of the conceptual art derived from the British Arts and Language movement, which were expounded in art schools in Great Britain in the late 1970s. These artists also based their works on French Theory, in particular on notions of semiotics and 'deconstruction' formulated in the works of Michel Foucault, Jacques Derrida and Jean-François Lyotard, and the response to them by postcolonial scholars such as Homi B. Bhabha and Gayatri C. Spivak. Finally, they were nourished and developed with the help of the theoretical tools proposed within cultural studies – generated by *race, class and gender'* – by the team at the CCCS (Centre for Contemporary Cultural Studies) working around Stuart Hall.

Whilst the works of Chila Kumari Burman have been regularly shown in group exhibitions since 1985,[162] they seem to be particularly resistant to any institutional classification and therefore to any critical reception. They did not figure in either of the two major exhibitions organised by Rasheed Araeen: *The Essential Black Art*—a show that defined its own terms—at the Chisenhale Gallery (1988), or the historical *The Other Story* at the Hayward Gallery (1989). Nor were they exhibited in *Migrations* at the Tate Britain. However, her works have been regularly shown in the exhibitions organised by the artists and curators from Black Art, such as *The Thin Black Line* at the Institute of Contemporary Art (1985), *Along the Line of Resistance* at the Rochdale Gallery (1989), *Transforming the Crown* at the Studio Museum (1997). My book is voluntarily positioned in terms of a political, non essentialist and pluri-ethnic definition of Black Art, and artists and writers like susan pui san lok have highlighted the specific, uncomfortable position of Asian British artists within British Black Art.[163] Chila Kumari Burman's works are regularly associated with

[162] Keen Melanie and Elizabeth Ward, *Recordings,* op. cit., p. 56.
[163] Susan Pui San Lok, "A to Y (Entries for an inventiony of Dented "I"s)", in *Shades of Black,* op.cit. , p.59-66

Indianness and contemporary Asian art, and as such they are part of British Black Art. Her works propose a reading of the cultural and political history in Great Britain from the counter-culture movements of the 1970s to the paradigms of cultural globalisation in the 1990s.

Dick Hebdige, one of the theorists of cultural studies, observes the coexistence in the summer of 1976 of punk rock and the Notting Hill festival (which he analyses as the expression of Rastafarianism by reggae), in other words, two expressions of 'sub-culture'. He interprets this phenomenon as one of the tools of globalism and of the massification of music culture. Hebdige builds his analysis on the convergences of black and punk music cultures in their transgressive forms based on the unifying principle of popular culture. To accomplish this objective, he traces the genealogy of reggae in the West Indies and demonstrates that the popular youth 'white' culture was elaborated in response to the different waves of immigration in Great Britain and in the United States: 'Punk reproduced the entire sartorial history of post-war working-class culture in "cut form", combining elements which had originally belonged to completely different epochs.'[164] Reggae, 'sound system', and punk share a preference for the street, the pub, and the local neighbourhood. According to Dick Hebdige, the proletarian characteristics and the recourse to obscenity and arrogance of punk culture, reveal a marginal, subservient, minority identity. At that time, reggae was seducing the punks, who were seeking to give meaning to their social alienation, and recognised in the Rastafarian heritage a kind of solidarity and radicality that was of interest to them:

> This parallel white 'ethnicity' was defined through contradictions. On the one hand it centred, however iconoclastically, on traditional notions of Britishness (the Queen, the Union Jack, etc.). It was local. It emanated from the recognizable locales of Britain's inner cities. It spoke city accents. And yet, on the other hand, it was predicated upon a denial of place. It issued out of nameless housing estates, anonymous dole queues, slums-in-

[164] Dick Hebdige, *Subculture, The Meaning of Style,* (1979), New York, London, Routledge, 2005, p. 26.

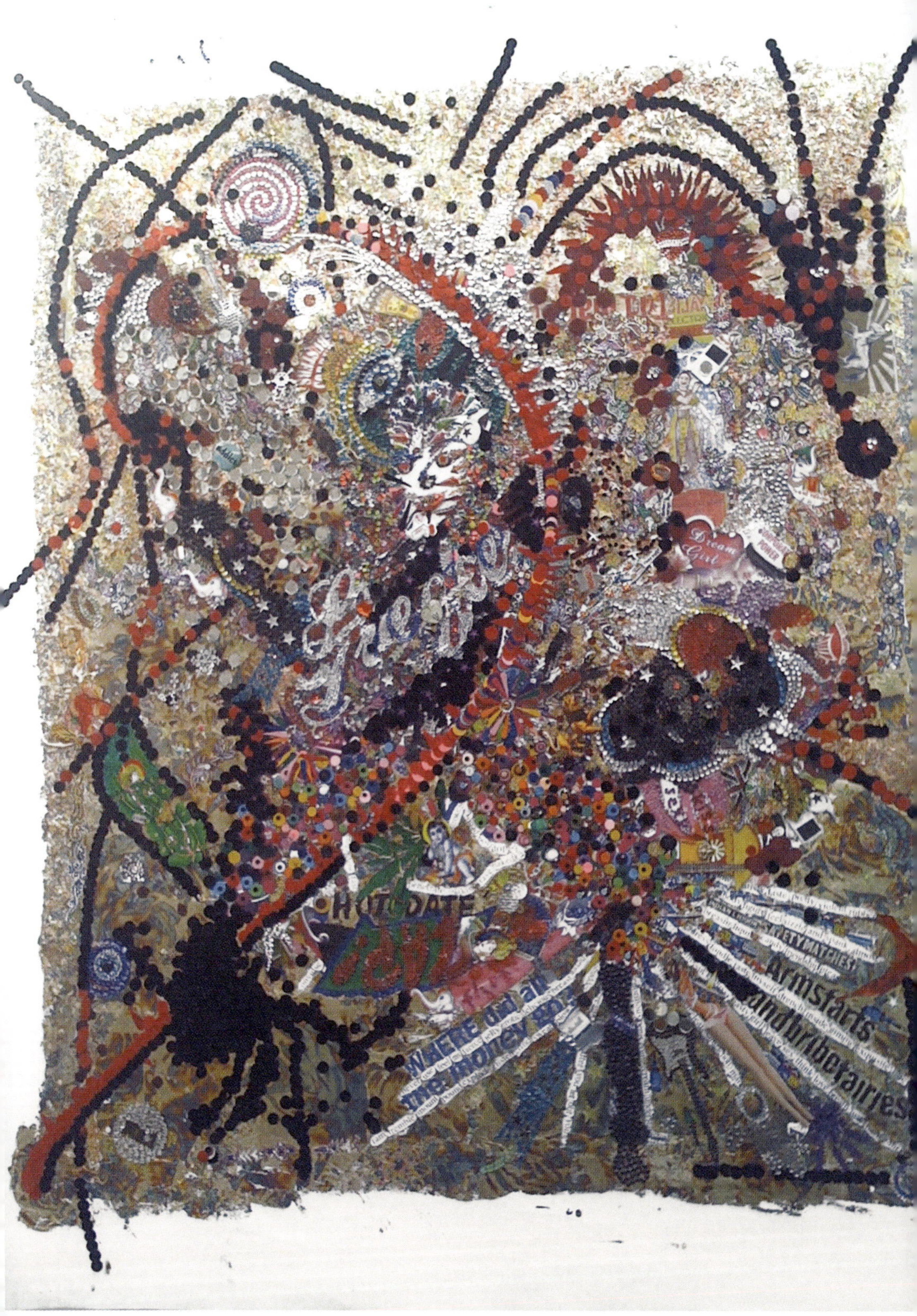

the-abstract. It was blank, expressionless, rootless. This punk subculture can be contrasted against the West Indian style which had provided the basic models. Whereas urban black youths could place themselves through reggae 'beyond the pale', in an imagined elsewhere (Africa, the West Indies), the punks were tied to present time. They were bound to a Britain which had no foreseeable future.[165]

Isaac Julien continued the work of the Blk Art Group and was the Director of the Sankofa Film and Video Collective, with which he developed an expressionist documentary aesthetic, used in *Young Soul Rebels* in 1991. In this film, he explicitly shows the links between the punk and reggae movements under Thatcher, seven years after his film *Territories* (1984), an expressionist documentary on the Notting Hill carnival. Likewise, the use of the flag by the artists associated with the Young British Artists, such as Tracey Emin and Chris Ofili, can in this light be apprehended in the tradition of the Sex Pistols singing "God Save The Queen". The same is true when they hold up the Union Jack whilst Jamie Reid cleverly reappropriates Cecil Beaton's portrait of the queen by adding touches of Situationism in the midst of May 1968 — an amulet used both to blindfold her and as a gag to silence her.

Contrary to the distinctions and categories proposed by Dick Hebdige, I would like to insist on the embedded nature of the cultural motifs within the artistic productions, particularly in those of Chila Kumari Burman. In *Dad on Ship Coming to Britain and Three Queens,* 1995 (Fig.14), she juxtaposes a portrait of her mother, a 5 pound note, the face of Queen Elisabeth, and her self-portrait (the 3 queens), and adds a photograph of her father leaning on a bar counter and one of his ice cream truck taken at Freshfield Beach in 1976. The rituals around Queen Elisabeth II remain vivid and popular.[166] The bank note is a

---

[165] Ibid. p. 65.

[166] From 1870 to 1914, the rituals of the monarchy became simple and popular, whilst Queen Victoria withdrew from the political affairs of the nation. Their aims tended to strengthen the symbolic influence of the Crown. In 1877, she was proclaimed Empress of India. After 1988, London installed numerous commemorative statues. While in Russia, Germany, Italy, the United States and Austria heads of State were the focus of ceremonial events, England promoted its monarch. Likewise, the symbols of the monarchy started being marketed, on porcelain dishes, cups and medals.

Fig.21 Chila Burman *My Hot Date*, 2013.
127 x 98 cm Canvas, rhinestones, bindis, diamond dust, Indian body Stickers, Diamantes, Swarowski pearls, fridge magnets, Vajazzling body crystals.

quintessential item of communication and exchange, which when adjusted to the face of a South Asian woman, creates an immediate reference to the history of imperialism. The moral, political and religious governance of the monarchy of the Queen Mother is associated with her representation on the bank note and with the construction of the British Empire. The bank note, which appears as a watermark in the portrait of the artist's mother, is the back of the 10 pound note, bearing the effigy of Charles Dickens. The *Pickwick Papers* (1836-1837) were commissioned by the caricaturist Robert Seymour, and these short stories relate the adventures of a member of the Nemrod club in London against the backdrop of a critique of social justice. Charles Dickens represents cricket and the English spirit.[167] Her father's travelling ice cream cone shop would become a recurrent subject in the work of Chila Kumari Burman, particularly via her critique of advertising imagery. This imagery was elaborated in relation with the internationalist positions of the avant-garde in the Dada movement and Kurt Schwitters.[168] Indeed, lithography, etching and printing material predominate in her work, techniques inherited from the artistic avant-garde and the propaganda poster in Socialist Europe.

The artistic tools and materials used by Burman and her theoretical knowledge and political culture all developed during her training in Leeds, as well as in the autodidactic process in which she engaged during her stay there. She learned and accumulated knowledge by meeting different people. For instance, she mentions her exchanges with a Yugoslavian Marxist reader of *Socialist Challenge*.[169] Burman's outlook was also shaped by feminist movements such as the Leeds Asian Women's Refuge in 1981, which was in the same sphere as the magazine *Mukti*. She listened to a variety of music ranging from Bob Marley to Bob Morrison, including the blues; she also read Afro-

[167] The bank note used by Chila Kumari Burman went out of circulation in 2003, and Dickens was replaced by Charles Darwin.
[168] Rina Arya, *Chila Kumari Burman, Shakti, Sexuality and Bindi Girl*, London, KT Press, 2012, p. 26.
[169] My interview with Chila Kumari Burman, at Rich Mix, London, 21 April 2015.

Caribbean poetry. The Sex Pistols and the Clash came to play in Leeds. It was the political culture of the times that occupied her evenings. She participated in the Rock and Racism concerts, read the New Musical Express. and took interest in the feminist positions of Simone de Beauvoir, attended numerous feminist conferences in Leeds and went to the Black and Asian Conferences organised by the Organisation for Women of Asian and African Descent in Leeds, and then in London:

> When I was in Leeds, Griselda Pollock ran the history of art department. However I was in the polytechnic. All the students of the university used to come down to Polytechnic. (…) All the artists doing political work wanted to meet us because we were talking about class, because we were more working class.[170]

Different punk-anarchist, poster-collage, Caribbean reggae, Marxist, antinuclear and feminist-academic artistic and cultural practices were superimposed, and Stuart Hall was a friend of Mike Fitzgerald, who was the partner of Burman's sister at that time. The following year at the Slade School of Art, Burman met Stanley Jones her tutor who worked in the Printmaking Department. Slade had very close relations with certain 'community printers', particularly with the Poster Film Collective.[171] Print workshops were generally a forum for radical thought in Britain: The Red Women's Workshop, the Onlywomen Press, Women in Print, as well as Lenthall Road and the Poster Workshop.[172] When I visited Chila Kumari Burman's studio in 2015, I perceived in her boxes of books Ways of Seeing by John Berger, Introduction to Marxism by Ernest Mandel and a 1998 issue of Mix, the Magazine of Artist-Run Culture. This mixture of books gives us a glimpse of the foundations of her artistic practices, which combine lithography, photolithography and *photoengraving*.

These superimpositions of tools and cultural references explain the wide variety of artistic choices, and how they were

[170] Ibid.
[171] Peter Dunn, "Poster Film Collective", in Carol Kenna, Lynne Medcalf and Rick Walker (eds.), *Printing is Easy… ?* London, Greenwich Mural Workshop, 1986.
[172] Carol Kenna (ed.), *Printing is Easy… ?,* op. cit.

inscribed in different artistic affiliations. Certain works refer to the techniques of Yves Klein since his prints of female bodies (*Body Print* (1987) in acrylic paint and glitter, or the photographs in a Shotokan kimono (*Self-Portrait,* (1993). Others draw on the tools of activism, from her murals (including the one created with Keith Piper in 1986), to drawings like *No More Hiroshima* (1979), in which two faces don masks and bombs, and the lithography *If There is No Struggle, There is No Progress – Uprisings,* (1981), a map of the 1981 revolts in Britain.

SHARED POLITICAL CULTURES FROM "RACE, CLASS, GENDER" TO "BLACKNESS"

New generations of artists came to supplement British Black Art. First of all, those who were a bit too quickly categorised as Young British Artists. Some exploited the material offered by identity-based politics while proposing to take into consideration the neoliberal shift and the entrepreneurial and individualistic politics under Thatcher. However, some artists such as Jeremy Deller, Richard Billingham and Mark Wallinger cannot be read from that point of view. Their appropriation of the tools of "race, class and gender" bear witness in particular to their belonging to a transnational diasporic culture and/or the interest for popular cultures and the disappearance of the working class by some artists who reuse the symbolic repertory of the revolutionary motifs from punk-anarchist movements, trade unions and the multi-referential left known as the New Left.

Social photography was also gaining in importance and becoming highly visible at that time. It was grounded in photography that depicts the customs and social inequalities of British society – of which Bill Brandt and Homer Sykes had been the paragons since the 1930s –, as well as in the tradition of community photography, which was practiced in the 1970s in artistic workshops such as the Hackney Flashers, and Half Moon Photography. These community workshops embraced the causes of popular education and were often associated with '*do it yourself*' practices, in particular print making, collage and silkscreen. For instance, the Poster/Film Collective welcomed students from the Slade School of Fine Art, such as Jonathan Miles. These workshops supported trade unionists and those who demonstrated against racism.[173] The BLACKWOMANPRINTPROJECT was held in 1988 and displayed the results of a workshop, whilst Rock Against Racism was also very active.[174]

How can we understand the transmission and circulation of certain motifs in the 1990s within different artistic productions? We must reflect on the precise role played by the cultural studies project and on the breaking up of the left as a point of articulation between the artistic scenes in the 1990s. What is the mechanism behind its obviously political appropriation and dissemination in the form of depoliticized culture?

First of all, cultural studies are not a homogeneous *discipline*, rather they were built in reaction to the break-up and then complete overhaul of left wing parties in Britain, and they disseminated critical theory in a viral way. In "Life and Times of the First New Left",[175] Stuart Hall writes about the multiple heritages of the New Left. In the 1950s, Oxford University welcomed members of the communist party including Raphael Samuel and Peter Sedgwick, representatives of the Fabian Society and independents, who would meet and discuss at the Socialist Club.

Hall makes a distinction between two traditions: the first – associated with the journal the *New Reasoner*, based in Yorkshire, in the industrial north of Great Britain –, brought together Edward Thompson, John Saville, Christopher Hill, and Eric Hobsbawm; the second constitutes a modernist, cosmopolitan axis (Oxford, London), and was associated with the journal *Universities and Left Review*

---

[173] John A. Walker, *Left Shift, Radical Art in 1970s Britain,* London, New York, I.B.Tauris, 2002, p.161.

[174] Paul Gilroy, *There ain't no Black in the Union Jack,* op. cit.

[175] Stuart Hall, "Life and Time of the First New Left", in *New Left Review 61,* Jan-Feb. 2010, p. 177-196. In 2010, Hall explained more clearly the multiple currents that shaped the formation of the New Left in the 1950s in Oxford, which were in response to two moments in history: the crushing of the Hungarian Revolution by the Soviets and the French and British invasion of the Suez Canal.

(1957-1959). These different left-wing groups met at the New Left Club in London to discuss topics such as nuclear disarment, popular culture, the Third World, and the race riots in Notting Hill in 1958. As a result, the humanist socialism of Edward Thompson and the progressive socialism of Raymond Williams came together in the journal edited by Stuart Hall, the *New Left Review*, until 1962, the date at which Perry Anderson and Tom Nairn turned back to Antonio Gramsci and a more radical Marxism. It was during this second phase of the *New Left* that Edward Thompson and Stuart Hall went to Birmingham to found *cultural studies* in the affiliation of Raymond Williams *Culture and Society* (1958)[176], Richard Hoggart *The Use of Literacy* (1957),[177] and E.P. Thompson *The Making of the English Working Class* (1963)[178]—in short, the materialist tradition. However, it would take several more years for the CCCS to appropriate the texts of Michel Foucault, Antonio Gramsci, Feminist theoreticians, the Frankfurt School, and identity-based theories, within a transdisciplinary approach. The political climate within the different left-wing groups in Britain, the international context with the cold war, and the interest of activists on the left for education and the arts shaped the writing on social classes in terms of what was called *agency*.[179]

According to Roger Bromley, *Policing the Crisis* by Richard Hoggart (1978) puts an end to a certain nostalgic era of cultural studies, which would then develop within feminist studies and texts on race, ethnicity, and more generally the struggles of 'black people'.[180] This shift is obvious in *The Empire Strikes Back, Race and Racism in 70s Britain* (1982),[181] to which Kobena Mercer attributes critical authority because:

[176] Raymond Williams, *Culture and Society,* (1958), New York, Columbia University Press, 1983.

[177] Richard Hoggart, *The Use of Literacy, Aspects of Working-class Life with Special Reference to publications and Entertainments*, London, Penguin, 1957.

[178] Edward Palmer Thompson, *The Making of the English Working Class,* (1963), New York, Vintage Books, 1966.

[179] I refer to the term proposed by Alfred Gell in his 1998 book *Art and Agency*, translated into French by the term 'agentivité', which has been the subject of debate.

[180] Roger Bromley, introduction to the chapter "Cultural Studies in Britain", in Jessica Munns and Gita Rajan, *A Cultural Studies Reader, History,Theory, Practice*, London, New York, Longman, 1995, p. 152.

[181] CCCS, *The Empire Strikes Back, Race and Racism in 70s Britain,* (1982), London, Center for Contemporary Cultural Studies, London, Routledge, 1992.

[…] it helped to effect a major paradigm shift from race-relations sociology to cultural studies, which in turn, actively contributed to the new forms of artistic practice in film, art and photography. The new generation of black intellectuals who were writing, such as Pratibha Parmar, Paul Gilroy, Hazel Carby and Errol Lawrence, helped displace the theory/ practice dichotomy by bringing activist experience to bear on the production of 'really useful knowledge' within the academic world, creating a toolbox of resources capable of all sorts of uses.[182]

We have already seen that the first official relations between Stuart Hall and Black Art date back to the paper "New Ethnicities" read by Hall at the Black Film, British Cinema Conference organised by Kobena Mercer at the Institute of Contemporary Art. Indeed, British Black Art also has its roots in a humanism, Marxism, Poststructuralism and Feminism that was coming to terms with postmodernism.[183]

In addition, at the end of the 1980s, these different cultures comprising the New Left were irrigating the different cultural scenes and enable us to establish their affiliations. Certain artists categorised by institutions as Black Art, Young British Artists and photographers shared a common preoccupation: the social and cultural history of urban environments. The artists from British Black Art attached it to propositions that defined a diasporic 'home' as proposed by cultural studies – Stuart Hall (and postcolonial studies – Homi Bhabha – and anthropology – James Clifford) – within the New Left, whilst the artists known as Young British Artists were playing with the references of 'Englishness' (derived from the conservative current and endowed with new significations by Margaret Thatcher) while renovating it with the help of new "subjects" borrowed from cultural studies.

Numerous artists – placed in the margins of Young British Artists, or associated with the photographic practices of British Black

---

[182] Kobena Mercer, "The Cultural Politics of Diaspora", in *Welcome to the Jungle, New Positions in Black Cultural Studies,* New York, London, 1994, p. 13.

[183] Fredric Jameson, *Postmodernism or the Cultural Logic of Late Capitalism* (1991) and David Harvey, *The Condition of Postmodernity* (1989). This break with the beginnings of cultural studies can be seen in the articles in the special issue of *Journal of Communication Inquiry* dedicated to Stuart Hall (*Journal of Communication Inquiry* 10 (2), 1986).

Art, or linked to photography schools in northern Great Britain working on social documentaries in the materialist tradition (Amber Collective, Paul Graham) – chose to depict the end of industrialization and the beginning of the service society. At the same time, other artists were focusing on the history of folklore and tourism (Jeremy Deller, Paul Reas, Patrick Keiller), drawing on the left-wing critical tradition associated with Raphael Samuel.

By focusing on three works that are representative of these different scenes in the 1990s, we may observe their similarities in terms of political culture. First, the photographic traditions of the social documentary that draw on the heritage of Raphael Samuel. The first photograph in the series *Flogging a Dead Horse, The Great Northern Experience* (1993), by Paul Reas: *The Man With the Movie Camera* (Fig.19), who is associated with documentary photography, ironically refigures the name of an amusement park in Beamish, in Durham. A man in the foreground, with his eye on his camera, is filming a scene miming the industrial past of Newcastle, which is presented as a reconstitution of its streets and shops, oriented diagonally in the image. The tourists are weighted down with cameras and backpacks, strolling behind the empty cart of a local beer producer. The past is re-enacted, filmed and recorded by the onlookers. The tour, walk or stroll takes place in memory, which is itself recomposed by actors in a theatre. It apes the history of a 'past up for sale'.[184] In response to the declining industrial activity and the closing of factories, this kind of tourism expanded greatly in the 1980s, and the unemployed miners became actors who played their former roles in history (*Redundant miner now employed to show tourists around the coal face he once worked,* North East England, 1993). This decade marks the beginning of a rediscovery of the past and praise for it that is visible in British cinema with the development of costume films, like *Howards End* (1992).[185] Raphael Samuel has closely analysed the relationship between

[184] Ibid.*"The past is up for sale."*
[185] This film is an adaptation of E.M. Forster's novel, *Howards End* (1910), about social classes in the early 20th century. It was directed by James Ivory. Henri Walcox was played by Anthony Hopkins and Margaret Shlegel was embodied by Emma Thompson.

cinema and heritage in his book *Theatre of Memories.*[186] In his article "Resurrectionism",[187] he lists the different ways in which the past was resurrected, over various periods and in all fields of art. What Frederic Jameson has called the 'nostalgia for the present'[188] or the fear of time passing, which engulfs the present, is expressed by a historicization of cities (he cites the Merchant City[189] district in Glasgow as an example), and especially a museumification of industrial life, the most controversial example of which is Beamish Hall, the amusement park of Durham[190] first imagined in 1958. Raphael Samuel identifies the 1960s as the time at which this attraction for historicization emerged in Britain. In opposition to the growing modernisation of urban and rural life, the taste for folklore, tradition, memory, and genealogy was welcomed. For instance, flea markets and antique dealers provided an alternative to the consumer society that was emerging at a large scale. Anxiety was mounting in response to the changing rural landscape, and the country houses or cottages had to be preserved and the villages kept intact.[191]

Associated with Black Women Artists, Ingrid Pollard is a photographer who in a similar approach relates the history of immigrants within the 'green and pleasant land'[192] and national history. In *Seaside, 1989* (Fig.17), she worked close to the sea. This installation combines self-portraits and postcards with tourist souvenirs such as ashtrays and beer mugs featuring the effigy of Hastings. Ingrid Pollard adds a comment under each postcard: '1066 a date remembered throughout the world as marking the final invasion of Britain' or '… "and what part of Africa do you

[186] Raphael Samuel, *Theatres of Memory*, London, Verso, 1994.
[187] Raphael Samuel, "Resurrectionism", in David Boswell and Jessica Evans (eds.), *Representing the Nation: A Reader,* New York, Routledge, Open University, 2005, p.163.
[188] Fredric Jameson, *Postmodernism, or The Cultural Logic of Late Capitalism*, Durham, Duke University Press, 1991.
[189] Certain streets in Glasgow were resurfaced as in pre-industrial times. In "Resurrectionism", *op.cit.*, p. 168, Raphael Samuel adds: '*Exorcizing memories of the shipyards by resurrecting the commercial glories of the Age of Adam Smith, while at the same time providing a showcase for modern fashion and a new business headquarters for information technology*.'
[190] Beamish Hall is a 120-hectare amusement park designed by Frank Atkinson and built 1970.
[191] It is the Civic Trust in the 1950s and 1960s that would be officially ratified in 1967 by the Civic Amenities Act, which confers powers upon local authorities to designate lad nd to be protected.
[192] This expression is from William Blake's poem *Jerusalem*.

come from?" inquired the walker'. The city of Hastings, which is now a very popular place for tourism in England, is first of all a territory of immigration. The eponymous battle opposing William the Conqueror and King Harold Godwinson is linked here to Enoch Powell's 'Rivers of Blood' speech, which explicitly calls for the return of immigrants from the Commonwealth to their place of origin. These transhistoric combinations evoke the colonisation of knowledge, and the reconquest of a diasporic and migratory British history. Her self-portrait as a young lady curled up on the pebbles is combined with a photograph of tea time with scones and clotted cream. The feeling of solitude and sadness emanating from these images is short-circuited by the ridiculously kitsch touristic objects she inserts in her compositions, which include three white chocolate sea shells in a scallop shell, labelled 'A gift from Hastings', a pink sucker in a wrapper bearing the image of a war ship, and postcards of Hastings featuring several images of the city against an orange background.

Based on his interest for history, tradition and the working class identity and local folklore, Jeremy Deller, often situated in the wake of the YBAs, proposed the exhibition *Folk Archive* (2000), which combined national events and regional cultural traditions. *Folk Archive* was a collaborative project carried out with the conceptual artist Alan Kane (Fig.20). It took seven years to bring together the material needed for a show of national folklore, and the result was a heterogeneous panorama of practices ranging from Arts and Crafts to a gurning festival,[193] and the making of banners for events. The two artists declared that 'with *Folk Archive* we are treading path between being artists and being anthropologists'.[194] The exhibition became a snapshot of festive Great Britain; a composition of rural traditions, and of the symbols of Britishness, from cake festivals to the Tea Festival and the Durham Miners' Gala. Jeremy Deller and Alan Kane are not the first contemporary artists to show interest in working class culture; the Amber Collective produced many films that 're-enact' or

[193] Tommy Mattinson, *World Gurning Champion,* Egremont, Cumbria, 2004.
[194] Jeremy Deller and Alan Kane, *Folk Archive*, London, Books Works, 2005, p. 2.

designate these traditions as the foundations of the community values[195] of working-class culture.

These works by Paul Reas, Ingrid Pollard and Jeremy Deller all discuss what the communist theorist Eric Hobsbawm calls 'the invention of tradition'[196] – in the margins of customs and heritage, when repetition and the process of commemoration are embellished through the production of a common object, rituals, toasts or speeches. In line with the tradition of anthems, flags and representations of John Bull, come regional effigies such as the tar barrels of Ottery St Mary[197] or the 'Burry Man' in Scotland.[198] According to Eric Hobsbawm, the traditions invented correspond to three types of events. The first 'establishing or symbolizing social cohesion or membership of groups'; the second 'establishing or legitimizing institutions, status or relations of authority'; whilst the aim of the third 'was socialization, the inculcation of beliefs, value systems and conventions of behaviours'.[199] Paul Reas re-enacts the life of the working class, Ingrid Pollard proposes a historiography of British history, and Jeremy Deller and Alan Kane bring together under the term 'folklore' all the popular practices, from protest marches against the war or ones demanding a reassessment of the status of prostitutes in relation to the Notting Hill Carnival, to the commemoration of the death of Princess Diana. These artists' graphic choices express their political positions with regard to both the definition of territory and a common cultural history.

The political identities debated by cultural studies as of the 1970s would become the tools shared by the different artistic scenes

[195] The film *The Scar* by Amber Collective (1997) depicts the Durham Miners' Gala as the place of an amorous encounter between the two principal protagonists.

[196] Eric Hobsbawn and Terence Ranger (eds.), *The Invention of Tradition*, Cambridge, Cambridge University Press 1983.

[197] Every 5 November since the 17th century, men, women and children march across the city of Ottery St Mary holding aloft a burning barrel.

[198] Every August in South Queensferry, Scotland, one of the inhabitants embodies the Burry Man. A man dressed in flannel is covered with the flowers or burrs of Burdock plants and parades around the streets. Homer Sykes has also photographed this event in his series *Once a Year*, cited above.

[199] Eric Hobsbawn,"Introduction: Inventing Traditions", *The Invention of Traditions,* op. cit, p. 9.

in the following decades. However, the different traditions that were so meaningful in the artistic productions of the 1980s—including the use of notions based on mass culture, the reference to British history, as well as the use of social figures and the introduction of notions linked to gender and sexuality—would become scandalous in the 1990s within certain artistic productions, like those of Tracey Emin, which reuse the same motifs but abandon their political content. For example, the reconfiguration of artistic categories in response to the break-up of the New Left becomes more problematic when it combines marginal or minority figures with that of the rioter, a theme developed by Rasheed Araeen, Keith Piper and Donald Rodney, as we saw earlier.

Likewise, in "Cultural Identity and Diaspora", Stuart Hall defines cultural identity in terms of two positions: one is essentialist and embodies a common homogeneous culture, whilst the other is constructivist. Hall argues that 'It's only from this second position that we can properly understand the traumatic character of the "colonial experience"',[200] which implies that the subject has a certain position in history, one that is fragile and singular, discontinuous. Furthermore, this position of enunciation, built by the Western thinking of 'the marginal, the underdeveloped, the periphery, the "other"'[201] was debated by those within British Black Art as well as by the Young British Artists. 'Race, class and gender' and the media specific to cultural studies become the themes explored by YBAs because they are the place of enunciation of a contextualised subject: 'We all write and speak from a particular place and time, from a history and a culture which is specific.'[202]

Let us take for example the coloured quilt *Remembering 1963* (2002) in which Tracey Emin tells the story of her mother's life in London, where she was assimilated with the 'new Blacks', as the black words against a red background suggest. In the middle of this quilt, figures a

[200] Stuart Hall, "Cultural Identity and Diaspora", op. cit, p. 225.
[201] Ibid., p. 228.
[202] Ibid, p. 222.

flag. Racial insults and Saint George's cross evoke the far-right, nationalist feelings in England. They spit on her[203] and called her a 'wog'.[204] Tracey Emin's mother claims she married a Turkish immigrant to exclude herself from the right-thinking middle class. The passage from identity politics to the representations of the motif of minorities in the work of Tracey Emin produces an image, a surface by means of the grid of a quilt. It is here, in the folds of a quilt, that the aforementioned irreconcilable scission occurs between motif and image, politics of the subject and place of enunciation. Whilst the 'Black' place of enunciation is appropriated by Tracey Emin, she withdraws from the New Left's project to overhaul the political system through cultural studies.

Cultural studies must therefore be understood as a common tool with which artists create in Great Britain. One that is well beyond the framework of British Black Art, but of which the content tends to be dissipated particularly in the 1990s, because of the arrival of new disciplines (Black studies, gender studies, postcolonial studies) and new objects of study, and also because of the end of the attempt to overhaul the political system, which was the central concern of Stuart Hall's project in the 1980s. The collapse of Communism in 1991, the arrival of *New Internationalism,* and the promotion of a transnational approach contributed to this dissipation. During this time, an American version of cultural studies tended to prevail,[205] in a way that was similar to the institutionalisation of African and African-American studies in the United States (since the 1960s and 70s), which imposed American Black Art on the international scene and a diasporic reading of artistic productions. The specific definition of the term 'Black' within the British context, which combines the political place of utterance of peoples of Afro-Caribbean and Asian origin within a demand for recognition within art history, lost its strength in the 1990s.

[203] Tracey Emin, *Strangeland,* London, Sceptre, 2005.
[204] A racial slur, mocked by Tracey Emin's mother, who capitalises its letters to create the expression: '*Western Oriental Gentleman*'.
[205] Annie Claustres, *Le Tournant populaire des Cultural Studies : L'histoire de l'art face à une nouvelle cartographie du goût (1964-2008),* Dijon, Les presses du réel, 2013.

It was replaced by transnational 'blackness' in the context of the debates on artistic globalisation that surfaced after 1989.

CHILA KUMARI BURMAN'S CRITIQUE OF B*LACKNESS*.

Chila Kumari Burman's artistic trajectory takes account of this shift. Her common point with her contemporaries is that she analyses the representations of *blackness*. This term is defined in as many ways as there are places in which it is used. For example, in France it is often associated with African diasporic thought, with Afro-American culture in the United States, whilst battling it out with the term 'British Asian' in Great Britain. Associated at times with a political project (Afrocentrism, Pan-Africanism, and black transnationalism), or a common musical, artistic or literary culture stemming from African diasporas, or the specificities linked to modern history and particularly to slavery, 'blackness' is a neologism used extensively starting in the 1990s to describe the rolling out of mass black culture. 'The Black experience', long represented in the figure of the situated artist in the works of Rasheed Araeen, Sonia Boyce and Keith Piper became either a deindividualized practice inscribed in an internationalist context – as in the works of Zarina Bhimji and Mona Hatoum –, or a discussion around the characteristics and popular stereotypes of blackness in the 1990s, which were highly influenced by the American model. Chris Ofili was inspired by pop culture and the ideology of black American militants in the 1960s and 70s, as well as by the new generation of thinkers who shaped British cultural studies, including Stuart Hall, Paul Gilroy and Homi K. Bhabha. The paintings *Sweet Popcorn* (1995) and *Afrodizzia* (1996) are the direct result of a combination of musical culture and the heritage of *blaxploitation*, an American cinema genre.[206] This cinema targeted an Afro-American audience, re-appropriating the stereotypes of the power wielded by

---

[206] I have already mentioned Isaac Julien's film on this subject.

the white middle class man, in a context marked by demands for civil rights. In this popular, excessive, erotic and violent cinema, the issues plaguing impoverished neighbourhoods, unemployment, family problems, corruption as well as racism all contribute to describing the daily lives of Americans. In 2002, Isaac Julien would produce a documentary film on blaxploitation called *BaadAsssss Cinema,* which continued his efforts to identify the major cultures of blackness, from the literary Harlem Renaissance of Langston Hughes – *Looking for Langston* (1989) – to the anti-colonialist theorist Frantz Fanon – *Black Skin, White Masks,* (1996). He alluded to *Sweet Sweetback's Baadasssss Song* (1971) by Melvin Van Peebles and *Shaft* by Gordon Parks (1971).[207] Inspired by similar references, Chris Ofili's large paintings with multiple coats of paint often feature collages of pairs of legs or buttocks cut out of pornographic magazines. *Pimpin' Ain't Easy* (1997) – offers the viewer a black make penis (2.43 × 1.82 m), rising up against a gold background, in which women's legs are juxtaposed with the haughty faces of Black Americans. The droplets of seminal liquid dispersed here and there form a constellation of silver and gold coins. Olifi also depicts Captain Shit, a superstar with an afro who is a quintessential representative of popular blackness. Elephant dung is used on his belt and shield, and even as a support for his inscriptions and the socle.

Meanwhile, when Chila Kumari Burman turned toward sexual imagery in the 2000s – *Be Careful Who You Sleep With* (2014) –, she juxtaposed the eroticised and sexist representations of women in commercial advertising with pornographic imagery; particularly by making use of the positions depicted in the *Kama Sutra*. Her practice, based on the accumulation of decorative elements, is comparable to Rococo techniques, a pile of pleasureful objects in a declining society. The hodgepodge mass of paint, colours, jewellery, pastilles, papers,

[207] The soundtracks were of high quality, with James Brown composing the one for *Black Caesar,* Isaac Hayes for *Shaft,* and Herbie Hancock for *The Spook Who Sat By the Door.*

114

words, sequins, and legs are reminiscent of the Baroque style developed by Chris Ofili in the erotic black masculine icons in his 'Captain Shit' series. Drawing, like the dotted line, is a permanent feature in Ofili and Burman's compositional practices.[208] In pop style, Chila Kumari Burman uses Indian figures found in the Punjabi calendars scattered around her family's house, and later bindis in *My Hot Date,* 2013 (Fig.21):

> The reason I started using bindis is that because none of my tutors ever made me look at Indian Art or Islamic Art, but only encouraged me to look at European Art. But my mum and my dad used to dress up and bought us fantastic outfits from India. We used bindis, bangles and everything.[209]

Based on the principle of accumulation, she produces icons that are close to Hew Locke's massive creations. In the tradition of Derek Jarman, who was inspired by Caravaggio, Isaac Julien depicts homoerotic figures draped in white, and contributed to the reflections on *'black masculinities'* before Thelma Golden made this theme the focus of the exhibition *Black Male.*[210] Rotimi Fani-Kayode and Alex Hirst proposed a series of Baroque portraits, in which the erotic beauty of the male body is figured in a chiaroscuro composition featuring cornucopias. Excess and a critique of authority characterise Chila Kumari Burman's *Venuses* in which artifice and decadence do not designate bourgeoisie, but rather the popular culture of kitsch. This art incorporates exhiberant decoration and also body decoration such as vajazzling body cristals. Along with the realist traditions of social fiction, her recourse to accumulation, *Arte Povera* and the staging of bodies links Chila Kumari Burman to other groups of artists in Europe, on the basis of a critique of stereotypical Indian imagery. Her specificity lies in the way she uses Pop, Rococo and Punk devices to critique sexist, erotic representations.

[208] However, in Chris Ofili's work the political citation remains hidden in the primer coat of the painting, just as the allusion to the murder of Stephen Lawrence in *No Woman No Cry* (1998), in which a black Madonna wails about a heinous and racist crime that was confirmed a few months later in the Macpherson report (1999).
[209] My interview with Chila Kumari Burman, op.cit.
[210] Thelma Golden (ed.), *Black Male, Representations of Masculinity in Contemporary American Art,* New York, Whitney Museum of American Art, 1994.

Blackness as the emphatic embodiment of Afro-American culture appealed to by the politics of gender and sex[211] is one of the points linking and opposing these different artistic propositions. On the one hand, the institutionalisation of Black studies particularly in the United States under the rubric of Afro-American art, or *diaspora studies,* unites the artists of the African diaspora in Africa, the United States, and the Caribbean with the British scenes. On the other hand, the demands for a mass black popular culture tends to dissolve the disparities or historical specificities that separate the history of slavery, and colonial and neocolonial history, in response to the demand for a popular internationalism. Perceived through the various filters of Afro-American universalist politics, anticolonial differentialist politics, ones in favour of cultural diversity, and finally internationalism, in Great Britain *blackness* evolved from its status as a counter culture derived from the Commonwealth to an undifferentiated transnational culture that was nonetheless integrated into curatorial, academic and scientific affairs. Chila Kumari Burman's artistic odyssey interrogates identity politics from a Marxist and Feminist differentialist position that emerged in the 1970s and affirmed a Black feminist critique (Black Feminism), in order to deconstruct the popular and virile form of Blackness especially in the USA.

[211] Isaac Julien is part of the collective Retake Cinema, which is very attached to gender studies and queer theories, whilst Chila Kumari Burman is affiliated with the feminist movements.

CONCLUSION

The artistic productions of Lubaina Himid, Eddie Chambers, Rasheed Araeen, Sonia Boyce and Chila Kumari Burman all strive to produce reflexive thoughts on Western art history in order to identify its internal aesthetic and ideological tensions.

My close analysis of the artistic productions themselves has enabled me to suggest new interpretations of emblematic works of British Black Art and to put into perspective the critical texts that accompany them. *Thin Black Line(s)* by Lubaina Himid clarifies the issues addressed by this artistic 'movement' and its methodology from the feminist point of view, which defines it as the creation of a discursive space. *Freedom and Change* by the same artist and *Destruction of the National Front* by Eddie Chambers show that it is precisely in the choice of artistic media that one can analyse the major issues at stake in the relations between the European avant-garde and the debates elicited by modernism that developed in the United States—after the reign of abstract expressionist painting—between pop art and conceptual art. *Paki Bastard* by Rasheed Araeen and *Three Legs Stuffed with Hair* by Sonia Boyce, further enact this thought concerning the presence not only of the body but of a subject that is situated, gendered, and has a sex and a race within the politics of otherness. The brutal shift in their practices is an illustration of how the subject takes on a position within conceptualism from Internationalism to New Internationalism. The works from *Dad on Ship Coming to Britain* (1995) to *My Hot Date* (2015) by Chila Kumari Burman figure the cultural fragmentation accompanying the break-up of the British left, from the project by the New Left to its disintegration. Bindis, the format, and the irony of her most recent works, set in motion a 'Black' political project for a political union of the diasporic artists living in the same territory, mocking the way in which the term now conveys a notion of 'Blackness' that is very porous and has marketing significations linked to the US model.

Since the end of the 1970s, the works I study have also engaged in the principal debates on art history, from the definition of modernism and the places in which it is rooted, to the shift in conceptual art, performance and then the return of painting, as well as in the history of ideas, from Poststructuralism to postcolonial studies.

Indeed, each of the emblematic works I analyse in this book develops a modus operandi or an artistic strategy based on the notion of *gap* or *differance*. In this process, they create a critical space for the major trends in terms of the artistic media used, gestures and discourses, which then become authoritative for art critics, the art market and museum institutions. Each of them challenges viewer expectations, and provide them with the tools they need to generate a commentary on art history in the West.

A similar set of questions characterised the debates around the 'global shift'[212] made by art historians between 1990 and 2000, because it required them to position themselves with respect to the philosophical project of modernity specific to Europe and its links with the construction of a canon of modern art and its multiple heritages in contemporary art. As a result, some call for the renewal of the universalist project of a world art history by extending the geographic

[212] Romain Bertrand, "Histoire globale, histoires connectées : un 'tournant historiographique'?" in Alain Caillé and Stéphane Dufoix, *Le 'tournant global' des sciences sociales*, Paris, La Découverte, 2013, p. 44-66.

boundaries of art, whilst others on the contrary, argue in favour of rehabilitating the marginalised artistic corpus within existing canons.[213] The methodological approach is obviously central.[214] It suggests the impossible combat to revise the canon and redefine artistic categories at the same time. For instance, Partha Mitter proposes to move beyond the tradition found in European-American art history and theory and its "universalist" canon within an epistemological framework that goes back to the Enlightenment',[215] whilst Luis Camnitzer proposes a reassessment of conceptualism through Tupamaros movements,[216] or based on the pedagogical practices of Simón Rodríguez, which employ new artistic genealogies.

Just as art historians are striving to find solutions for rewriting art history based on a process of decentring modernism[217], the circulation and transfer of art, or even the study of non-Western artistic practices, the works of British Black Art reveal the porous nature of artistic categories within the history of European art, and shed light on

[213] Some of the reference works include James Elkins, Zhivka Valiavicharska and Alice Kim, (eds.) *Art and Globalization,* Pennsylvania, The Pennsylvania State University Press, 2010, and Jonathan Harris, *Globalization and Contemporary Art,* Padstow, Wiley-Blackwell, 2011.

[214] The references are too numerous to be fully developed here, but in France, exchanges are developing albeit principally between Western researchers. For example, the excellent spatial and transnational history of the arts laboratory 'Artl@s' directed by Béatrice Joyeux-Prunel (ENS Paris) works with Thomas DaCosta Kaufman (Princeton University, Princeton): Thomas DaCosta Kaufmann, Catherine Dossin, and Béatrice Joyeux-Prunel, eds. *Global Artistic Circulations and the History of Art*, Farnham, UK, Ashgate, 2015. Sarah Wilson also initiated a research project (Courtauld Institute, London) with Boris Groys (New York University, New York) in 2010-2011, on *Global Conceptualism.* Russell Ferguson, Martha Gever, Trinh T. Minh-ha, Cornel West, (eds.) *Out There, Marginalization and Contemporary Cultures,* London, New York, MIT, 1990.

[215] Kobena Mercer reassessed modernism based on 'transcultural visual studies' in his series *Annotating Art's Histories,* whilst others were attempting to define contemporary art in its globalised form (Hans Belting, Jonathan Harris) leaving behind the anticolonial and postcolonial literature that had redefined contemporary art in terms of its margins in the 1990s. Partha Mitter, "Decentering Modernism: Art History and Avant-Garde Art from the Periphery", *The Art Bulletin,* vol. 90, n°4, Dec. 2008, p. 532.

[216] Luis Camnitzer, *Conceptualism in Latin American Art: Didactics of Liberation,* Austin, University of Texas Press, 2007.

[217] Brent Hayes Edwards, *Practice of Diaspora: Literature, Translation, and the Rise of Black Internationalism,* Cambridge, Harward University Press, 2003. Tina Campt, *Other Germans: Black Germans and the Politics of Race, Gender, and Memory in the Third Reich,* Ann Arbor, University of Michigan Press, 2003.

heretofore ignored artistic affiliations. Numerous artworks associated to the British Black Art are in need of further analysis built on a methodology crossing cultural studies, Black feminism and strategic formalism. The results of the different analysis of artworks associated with the term "black" within the UK context invite to other studies from a common political space, such as forms of conceptualism within Migratory Europe.

BIBLIOGRAPHY

Adamson Glenn and Jane Pavitt (eds.), *Postmodernism, Style and Subversion, 1970-1990*, London, Victoria and Albert Museum Publishing, 2011.

Ait Ben Lmadani Fatima et Nasima Moujoud, « Peut-on faire de l'intersectionnalité sans les ex-colonisé-e-s ?», *Mouvements,* La Découverte, n°72, 2012, p.11-21.

Araeen Rasheed, "From Primitivism to Ethnic Arts", *Third Text,* vol. 1, n° 1, 1987, p. 6-25.

Araeen Rasheed, "Introduction: When the Chickens come Home to Roost", in *The Other Story: Afro-Asian Artists in Post-War Britain*, London, South Bank Centre, 1989. p. 9-15.

Araeen Rasheed, "New Internationalism, or the Multiculturalism of Global Bantustans", in Rasheed Araeen and Jean Fisher, *Global Visions, Towards a New Internationalism in the Visual Arts,* London, Kala Press, Iniva, 1994, p. 3-11.

Araeen Rasheed, "Paint it Black", *City Limits,* 13-19 August 1982, n. pag.

Araeen Rasheed, "The Artist as a post-colonial subject and this individual's journey towards the centre", in Catherine King (ed.), *Views of Difference: Different Views on Art,* London, New Heaven, The Open University, Yale University, 1999, p. 231-255.

Araeen Rasheed, "The Emergence of Black Consciousness in Contemporary Art in Britain: Seventeen Years of Neglected History", *The Essential Black Art,* Chisenhale Gallery, and Black Umbrella, 1988, n. pag.

Araeen Rasheed, « From Primitivism to Ethnic Arts », *Third Text,* vol 1, issue 1, 1987, p. 6-25.

Araeen Rasheed, « International Art, Eurocentrisme, Racism, Domination », *Studio International* n° 2, 1978.

Araeen Rasheed, Eddie Chambers, "Black Art: a discussion", *Third Text*, vol. 2, n° 5, 1988, p. 51-77.

Araeen Rasheed, *Making Myself Visible*, London, Kala Press, 1984.

Araeen Rasheen, (ed.), *The Other Story : Afro-Asian artists in Post-War Britain*. London, Hayward Gallery, 1989.

Araeen, Rasheed, (ed.) *The Essential Black Art,* London, Chisenhale Gallery, and Black Umbrella, Arts Council, 1988.

Arya Rina, Chila Kumari Burman, Shakti, Sexuality and Bindi Girl, London, KT Press, 2012.

Ascroft Bill, Gareth Griffiths and Helen Tiffin, *The Empire Writes Back, Theory and Practice in Post-colonial Litterature*(1989), London, New York, Routledge, 2002

Bailey David A., Ian Baucom, and Sonia Boyce *Shades of Black, Assembling Black Art in 1980s Britain,* Durham, Duke University Press, Iniva, Aavaa, 2005.

Bailey David. A. et Stuart Hall Ten 8, *A Critical Decade*, vol 2, n° 3, 1992.

Bailey David. A., « Photographic Animateur, The photographs of Rotimi Fani-Kayode in relation to Black photographic practices », *Third Text*, n° 13, 1991, p. 57-62.

Bailey, David A et Kobena Mercer (eds.), *Mirage: Enigma of race and desire,* London, ICA et Iniva, 1995.

Baker Houston A., Jr, Manthia Diawara and Ruth H. Lindeborg, *Black British Cultural*

Studies, Chicago and London, The University of Chicago Press, 1996.

Baraka Amiri (LeRoi Jones), *Black Magic Poetry 1961-1967,* New York, The Bobbs-Merrill Co, 1969.

Barber, Ed (ed.), *Ten 8, Restricted Practices,* n° 7/8, 1982.

Bayer Jonathan and Alex Noble (eds.), *Images and Exploration, Some Directions in British Photography 1980/ 1985*, London, The Photographers Gallery, 1985.

Bayly C.A., *La Naissance du monde moderne (1780-1914)*, 2004, Paris, éditions de l'Atelier, 2007.

Beauchamp-Byrd Mora et Franklin M. Sirmans, *Transforming the Crown: African, Asian and Caribbean Artists in Britain 1966-1996*, New York, Caribbean Cultural Center, Unviversity of Chicago Press, 1997.

Bellmer Hans, *Petite anatomie de l'image*, Paris, Allia, 2010.

Berger John, *Ways of Seeing,* London, Penguin, 1972.

Bertrand Romain, "Histoire globale, histoires connectées : un 'tournant historiographique'?" in Alain Callé and Stóphane Dufoix, "Le 'tournant global' des sciences sociales", Paris, La Découverte, 2013, p. 44-66.

Betterton Rosemary, *Intimate Distance, Women, Artists and the Body,* London, New York, Routledge, 1996.

Bhabha Homi, *The Location of Culture,* New York, London, Routledge, 1994.

Bilge Sirma, "Intersectionality Undone", *Du Bois Review,* 2, 10, 2013, p. 405-424.

Brett Guy, *Exploding Galaxies: The Art of David Medalla*, London, *Third Text*, 1995.

Bromley Roger, "Cultural Studies in Britain", in Jessica Munns and Gita Rajan, *A Cultural Studies Reader, History, Theory, Practice*, London, New York, Longman, 1995, p. 149-153.

Bryce Jane, "Features", in Arts Reviews, 16 January, 1990.

Buchloh Benjamin, "Allegorical Procedures: Appropriation" (1982), version revised in Alexander Alberro and Sabeth Buchmann, *Art After Conceptual Art,* London, Vienna, MIT Press/Generali Foundation, 2006, p. 27-52.

Buchloh H.D., "Conceptual Art 1962-1969: From the Aesthetic of administration to the Critique of Institutions, *October,* vol. 55, 1990, p.105-143

Camnitzer Luis, *Conceptualism in Latin American Art: Didactics of Liberation,* Austin, University of Texas Press, 2007.

Camnitzer Luis, Jane Farver and Rachel Weiss, *Global Conceptualism: Points of Origin, 1950s-1980s,* New York, Queen Museum of Art, 1999.

Campt Tina, *Other Germans: Black Germans and the Politics of Race, Gender, and Memory in the Third Reich*, Ann Arbor, University of Michigan Press, 2003.

Carby Hazel V., « White Women Listen ! Black Feminism and the Boundaries of Sisterhood », in Houston A Baker, *Black British Cultural Studies,* London, New York, Routledge, 1997, p. 61-86.

CCCS (eds), *The Empire Strikes Back, Race and Racism in 70s Britain,* (1982), London, Centre for Contemporary Cultural Studies, Routledge, 1992.

Chambers Eddie (ed.), *Black Art: Plotting the Course*, Oldham, England, Oldham Art Gallery, 1988.

Chambers Eddie (ed.), *Black People and the British Flag,* Leicester, England, City Gallery, 1993.

Chambers Eddie, « His catechism, the Art of Donald Rodney », *Third Text*, n° 44, 1998, p. 43-54.

Chambers Eddie, *Black Artists in British Art: A History since the 1950s*, New York, I.B. Tauris, 2014.

Chambers Eddie, *Let the Canvas Come to Life with Dark Faces*, Coventry, Herbert Art Gallery, 1990.

Chambers Eddie, *Run through the jungle,* selected writings Iniva, notations n° 5, London, Iniva 1999.

Chambers Eddie, Tam Joseph and Junginda Lamba (eds), *The Artpack*, London, Haringey Arts Council, 1988.

Chambers Eddie, *Things Done Change: The Cultural Politics of Recent Black Artists in Britain*, Amsterdam, New York, Rodopi, 2012.

Cherry Deborrah (ed.), *Maud Sulter, Passion,* UK, Altitude Editions, 2015.

Claustres Annie, *Le Tournant populaire des Cultural Studies: L'histoire de l'art face à une nouvelle cartographie du goût (1964-2008),* Dijon, Les presses du réel, 2013.

Collette Christine F. and Keith Laybourn (eds.), *Modern Britain since 1979,* London, New York, I. E. Tauris, 2003.

Colley Linda, *Britons: Forging the Nation (1707-1837),* (1992), New Heaven, Yale University Press, 2009.

Cosgrove Stuart et Val Williams, (eds.), *Paul Reas, Flogging a Dead horse, Heritage Culture and its Role in Post-Industrial Britain,* Manchester, Cornerhouse, 1993.

Crenshaw Kimberle Williams, *Mapping the Margins: Intersectionality, Identity Politics, and Violence Against the Women of Color*, in, Martha Albertson Fineman, Rixanne Mykitiuk, (éds.), *The Public Nature of Private Violence*, New York, Routledge, 1994, p. 93-118.

Cubitt Sean, «Keith Piper, After Resistance, Beyond Destiny», *Third Text,* n°47, 1999, p.77-86.

DaCosta Kaufmann Thomas, Catherine Dossin, and Béatrice Joyeux-Prunel, (eds.), *Global Artistic Circulations and the History of Art,* Farnham, UK, Ashgate, 2015.

Deller Jeremy and Alan Kane, *Folk Archive,* London, Books Works, 2005.

Deller Jeremy, *The English Civil War II. Personnal Account of the 1984-1984 Miners'Strike,* London, Manchester, Artangel, Cornerhouse, 2002.

Doane Mary Ann, *Femmes Fatales, Feminism, Film Theory, Psychoanalysis,* London, Routledge, 1991.

Doy Gen, *Black Visual Culture: Modernity and Postmodernity*, London, I.B. Tauris, 2000.

Elkins James, Zhivka Valiavicharska and Alice Kim (eds.), *Art and Globalization*, Pennsylvania, The Pennsylvania State University Press, 2010.

Ellison Ralph, *Invisible Man*, New York, Random House, 1952.

Emin Tracey, *Strangeland*, London, Sceptre, 2005.

Fazakarley Jed, "Racism 'Old' and 'New' at Handsworth, 1985", in University of Sussex Journal of Contemporary History, n° 13, 2009-2010.

Ferguson Russell, Martha Gever, Trinh T. Minh-ha, Cornel West, (eds.), *Out There, Marginalization and Contemporary Cultures,* London, New York, MIT, 1990.

Fisher Jean (ed.), *Global Visions, Towards a New Internationalism in the Visual Arts, London,* Kala Press, Iniva, 1994.

Foster Hal, Rosalind Krauss, and Yve-Alain Blois, *Art since 1900, Modernism, Antimodernism, Postmodernism*, London, Thames and Hudson, 2004.

Foster Judith, *A Discussion of the relationship between Black Artists and British Art Institution*s, Bristol polytechnic, MA, 1991.

Fusco Coco, *Young, British and Black, a monograph on the work of Sankofa Film/Video Collective and Black Audio Film Collective,* Hallwalls, Contemporary Art Center, 1988.

Gavin Jantjes (ed.), *A Fruitful Incoherence, dialogues with artists on internationalism,* London, Iniva, 1998.

Gilbert & George, *For Aids,* London, Anthony d'Offay Gallery, 1989.

Gilroy Paul, « Art of Darkness : Black Art and the problem of belonging to England », *Third Text,* n° 10, 1990, p. 45-52.

Gilroy Paul, « Cruciality and the Frog's perspective, An agenda of difficulties for Black Arts Movements in Britain », *Third Text* n° 5, 1988, p. 33-45.

Gilroy Paul, *There Ain't no Black in the Union Jack,* London, Hutchinson, 1987.

Ginzburg Carlo, "Au-delà de l'exotisme : Picasso et Warburg", in *Rapports de force : histoire, rhétorique, preuve,* Paris, Le Seuil, Gallimard, 2003, p.101-116.

Golden Thelma (ed.), *Black Male, Representations of Masculinity in Contemporary American Art,* New York, Whitney Museum of American Art, 1994.

Gorz André, *Farewell to the Working Class : An Essai on Post-Industrial Socialism,* Pluto Press, London, 1982.

Grimley Terry, *Birmingham Post Art Review,* 1981 n. pag.

Gupta Sunil (ed.), *Disrupted Borders: An Intervention in Definition of Boundaries,* London, Rivers Oram Press, 1993.

Habermas Jürgen, *Philosophical Discourse of Modernity*, (1985), Cambridge, Polity Press, 1998.

Hall Stuart and Martin Jacques, *New Times, The Changing Face of Politics in the 1990s,* Lawrence & Wishart, London, 1989.

Hall Stuart, "Black Diaspora Artists in Britain: Three 'Moments' in Post-war History", History Workshop Journal, 2006, p.1-24.

Hall Stuart, "Assembling the 1980s: The Deluge and After," in Bailey David A., Ian Baucom, and Sonia Boyce *Shades of Black, Assembling Black Art in 1980s Britain,* Durham, Duke University Press, Iniva, Aavaa, 2005, p.1-20.

Hall Stuart, "Life and Time of the First New Left", *New Left Review 61*, Jan-Feb. 2010, p. 177-196.

Hall Stuart, « New Ethnicities » (1988), in David Morley and Kuan h Chen, *Critical Dialogues in Cultural Studies,* New York, Routledge, 1996, p. 442-451.

Hall Stuart, Chas Critcher, Tony Jeffeerson, John Clarke, and Brian Roberts (eds.), *Policing the Crisis: Mugging, the State and Law and Order*, London, the Macmillian Press, 1978.

Harris Jonathan, *Globalization and Contemporary Art,* Padstow, Wiley-Blackwell, 2011.

Harris Jonathan, *The New Art History, A Critical Introduction,* London and New York, Routledge, 2001.

Harvey David, *The Condition of Postmodernity* (1989), Cambridge, Oxford, Blackwell, 1992.

Hayes Edwards Brent, *Practice of Diaspora: Literature, Translation, and the Rise of Black Internationalism*, Cambridge, Harward University Press, 2003.

Hebdige Dick, *Subculture, The Meaning of Style,* (1979), New York, London, Routledge, 2005.

Hiller Susan, *The Myth of Primitivism*, London, New York, Routledge, 1991.

Himid Lubaina (ed.), *The Thin Black Line,* Hebden Bridge, Urban Fox Press, 1985.

Himid Lubaina et Pogus Ceasar (eds.), *Into the open : New Painting, prints and sculpture by contemporary Black Artists*, Sheffield, Sheffield Arts Departement, Mappin Art Gallery, 1984.

Hobsbawn Eric, Terence Ranger (eds), *The Invention of Tradition*, Cambridge, Cambridge University Press 1983.

Hoggart Richard, *The Use of Literacy, Aspects of Working-class Life with Special Reference to publications and Entertainments,* London, Penguin, 1957.

Hylton Richard, *The Nature of the Beast, Cultural Diversity and the Visual Arts Sector, A Study of policies, Initiatives and Attitudes 1976-2006,* Bath, ICIA, 2007.

Jameson Fredric, *Postmodernism, or The Cultural Logic of Late Capitalism,* Durham, Duke University Press, 1991.

Jantjes Gavin (ed.), *A Fruitful Incoherence: Dialogues with Artists on Internationalism,* London, Iniva, 1998.

Jantjes Gavin and Nicholas Serota (eds*.), From Two Worlds,* London, Whitechapel Gallery, 1986.

Johnstone Isabel (ed.), *Shock to the System: Social and Political Issues in Recent British Art from the Art Council Collection*, London, South Bank Centre, 1991.

Joseph Isaac and Yves Grafmeyer, *L'Ecole de Chicago, Naissance de l'écologie urbaine*, Paris, Flammarion, 1984.

Keen Melanie, Elisabeth Ward, (eds.): *Recordings: A Select Bibliography of Contemporary African, Afro-Caribbean and Asian British Art*, London, Iniva/Chelsea College of Art and Design, 1996.

Kenna Carol, Lyn Metcalf, et Rick Walker (eds.), Printing is easy... *Community Printshops 1970-1986?*, Greenwich Mural Workshop, 1986.

Khan Naseem, *The Arts Britain Ignores,* (1976), The Arts of Minorities in Britain, Commission for Racial Equality, 1981.

Kravagna Christian, « Towards a postcolonial art history of contact », *Text Zur Kunst,* «Globalismus Globalism », n° 23, sept. 2013, p. 110-131.

Lazarus Neil, *The Postcolonial Unconscious,* Cambridge, Cambridge, University Press, 2011.

Lejeune Anaël, Olivier Mignon and Raphaël Pirenne, (eds.), *French Theory and American Art*, Berlin, Sternberg, 2013.

Levine Caroline, "Scarled Up, Writ Small: a Response to Carolyn Dever and Herbert F. Tucker", *Victorian Studies,* vol. 49, n°1, 2006, p.100-105.

Levine Caroline, "Strategic Formalism: Toward a New Method in Cultural studies", *Victorian Studies*, vol. 48, n°4, 2006, p.625-657.

London, Victoria and Albert Museum Publishing, 2011.

Loomba Ania, *Colonialism/postcolonialism,* (1998), London, Routledge, 2005.

MacCorquodale Duncan, Naomi Siderfin, and Julian Stallabrass (eds.), *Occupational Hazard, Critical Writing on Recent British Art,* London, Black dog Publishing, 1998.

Mattinson Tommy, *World Gurning Champion,* Egremont, Cumbria, 2004.

Maud Sulter (ed*.), Passion: Discourses on Blackwomen's Creativity*, UFP, Hebden Bridge, 1990.

Mercer Kobena , « Black Art and the Burden of Representation », *Third Text,* n° 10, 1990, p. 61-78.

Mercer Kobena 'Perforations' conference paper in Reframing the Moment: Legacies of the 1982 Blk Art Group Conference held at the University of Wolverhampton on Saturday 27 October 2012, https://vimeo.com/76712100

Mercer Kobena, "Black art and the Burden of Representation", *Third Text,* n° 10, 1990, p. 61-78.

Mercer Kobena, "Ethnicity and Internationality, New British Art and Diaspora-Based Blackness", *Third Text,* n°49, winter 1999-2000, p. 51-62.

Mercer Kobena, "Iconography after Identity", in Bailey David A., Ian Baucom, and Sonia Boyce *Shades of Black, Assembling Black Art in 1980s Britain,* Durham, Duke University Press, Iniva, Aavaa, 2005, p.53-54.

Mercer Kobena, "Recoding Narratives of Race and Nation", in Mercer (et al.), *Black Film, British Cinema*, London, ICA, 1988, p.4-14.

Mercer Kobena, "The Cultural Politics of Diaspora", in *Welcome to the Jungle, New Positions in Black Cultural Studies*, New York, London, 1994, p. 1-32.

Mercer Kobena, « Black Art and the Burden of Representation », in *Welcome to the Jungle,* London, Routledge, 1994, p.233-258.

Mercer Kobena, *Cosmopolitan Modernisms*, London, Iniva, MIT, 2005.

Mercer Kobena, *Keith Piper: Relocating the remains*, London, Iniva, 1997.

Mercer Kobena, *Welcome to the jungle, New Positions in Black Cultural Studies*, London, Routledge, 1994.

Shapiro Meyer, Theory and *Philosophy of Art, Style, artist et society: selected papers,* New York, George Braziller, vol IV, 1994.

Mirza Heidi Safia (ed.), *Black British Feminism: A Reader*, London; New York, Routledge, 1997.

Mitter Partha, « Decentering Modernism : Art History and Avant-Garde Art from the Periphery », *The Art Bulletin*, vol.90, n° 4, dec 2008, p. 531-548.

Molesworth Helen (ed.), *This Will Have Been, Art, Love & Politics in the 1980s,* New Haven and London, Yale University Press, and Museum of Contemporary Art Chicago, 2012.

Molesworth Helen, "House Work and Art Work", *October,* vol. 92, 2000, p. 71-97.

Moulier Boutang Yann, *La révolte des banlieues ou les habits nus de la République*, Paris, Amsterdam, 2006

Mouvements, des idées et des luttes, « Ma cité a craqué, Dix ans après les révoltes urbaines de 2005 », n°83, 2015.

Munns Jessica and Gita Rajan (eds), *A Cultural Studies Reader, History, Theory, Practice*, New York and London, Longman, 1995.

Nead Linda, *Chila Kumari Burman, Beyond Two Cultures*, London, Kala Press, 1995.

Neverson Yvonne, "The Pan-Afrikan Connection", *Frontline Magazine*, 1982, n. pag.

Orlando (et al) « Globalisée, mondialisée, contemporaines. Pratiques, productions, et écritures de l'art aujourd'hui », *Les Cahiers du Musée national d'art moderne*, n°122, 2012-2013.

Orlando Sophie and Catherine Grenier (eds), *Art et Mondialisation*, Paris, Centre Pompidou, 2013.

Orlando Sophie, "Artistic categories and the Situation of Utterance: The period from 1989 to 1994 in Great Britain", *Critical Intervention,* Journal of African art history and visual culture, n°12, 2013, p. 6-19.

Orlando Sophie, "Sonia Boyce: Post- 1989 Art Strategies", *Critique d'art,* n°43, 2014, p.110-125.

Orlando Sophie, "Sonia Boyce: Sound, Tension and the Sacred", in *Scat-Sonia Boyce, Sound and Collabortaion,* Iniva, 2013, p.6-16.

Orlando Sophie, « What makes Britain So Great ? » La britannicité et l'art contemporain de 1979 à 2010 en Grande-Bretagne, supervised by Philippe Dagen, Paris 1 Panthéon-Sorbonne, and defended in 2010 at the INHA.

Owusu Kwesi, *Black British Culture and Society*, London and New York, Routledge, 2000.

Owusu Kwesi, *Storms of the Heart, An Anthology of Black Arts and Culture*, London, Camden Press, 1988.

Paige Abraham Julia Ann, *Transformation and Defiance in the Art Establishment: Mapping the Exhibition of the Blk Art Group (1981-1983),* M.Phil. Thesis, University of Birmingham, sept 2011.

Papastergiadis Nikos, *The Complicity of Culture: Hybridity and New Internationalism*, Manchester, Cornerhouse, n° 4, 1994.

Parker Roszika and Griselda Pollock, *Framing Feminism: Art and Women's Movement 1970-85,* London, Pandora, 1995

Piper Adrian, "The Logic of Modernism" (1993), *Callaloo,* vol 16 n°3, 1993, p. 574-578.

Piper Keith, « Introduction », *The Blk Art Group*, 3 Lindsey Walk, Hyson Green, Nottingham, ng7 6DJ, 1983, non pag. http://www.blkartgroup.info/index.html.

Pollard Ingrid, *Postcards Home,* London, Autograph ABP, 2003.

Pollock Griselda, *Differencing the Canon, Feminist Desire and the Writing of Art's Histories*, London, New York, Routledge, 1999.

Powell J. Richard and David Bailey, (eds.) *Rhapsodies in Black, Art of the Harlem Renaissance,* London, University of California Press, Hayward Gallery, 1997.

pui san lok susan, "A to Y (Entries for an inventiony of Dented "I"s)", in Bailey David A., Ian Baucom, and Sonia Boyce *Shades of Black, Assembling Black Art in 1980s Britain,* Durham, Duke University Press, Iniva, Aavaa, 2005, p. 59-66.

Reas Paul (ed.), *I can help*, Manchester, Cornerhouse, 1988.

Revel Judith « Ce que vaut la vie », *Multitudes,* n°27, 2006

Rhodes Colin, *Primitivism and Modern Art*, London, Thames and Hudson, 1994.

Roh Franz, *Postexpressionnisme — Réalisme magique — Problèmes de la peinture européenne la plus récente,* (1925), Dijon, Les Presses du réel, 2013.

Said Edward W., *Orientalism,* New York, Vintage Books, 1979.

Samuel Raphael, "Resurrectionism", in David Boswell and Jessica Evans (eds.), *Representing the Nation: A Reader*, New York, Routledge, Open University, 2005, p.163-184.

Samuel Raphael, *Theatres of Memory,* London, Verso, 1994.

Sivanandan Ambalavaner, "The Liberation of Black Intellectual", *Race and Class*, (vol.18), 1977, p. 329-343.

Spivak Gayatri C., "Can the Subaltern Speak" (1988), Rosalind Morris (ed), *Can the Subaltern Speak? Reflections on the History of an Idea*, New York, Columbia University Press, 2010, p.237-292.

Sulter Maud (ed.), *Passion: Discourses on Blackwomen's Creativity*, UFP, Hebden Bridge, 1990.

Tawadros Gilane (ed.), *Changing States, Contemporary Art and Ideas in an Era of Globalisation*, London, Iniva, 2004.

Tawadros Gilane, "Beyond the Boundary: The Work of Three Women Artists in Britain", *Third Text,* 8/9, 1989, p.121-150.

Tawadros Gilane, « Black women in Britain, A personal and Intellectual Journey », *Third Text,* n° 15, 1991, p. 71-76.

Tawadros Gilane, *Sonia Boyce, Speaking in Tongues*, London, Kala Press, 1997.

Thompson Edouard. P., *The Making of the English Working Class,* (1963), New York, Vintage Books, 1966.

Touraine Alain, "Le Retour de l'acteur", *Cahiers Internationaux de Sociologie*, Nouvelle série, Vol. 71, July-December 1981, p. 243-255.

Van Assche Christine (ed.), *Isaac Julien, Fantôme créole*, Paris, Baltimore livre 8, Centre George Pompidou, 2005.

Van Dijk Teun A., "Race, riots and the press: an analysis of editorials in the British press about the 1985 disorders", International Communication Gazette, vol. 43 no. 3, 1989, p. 229-253.

Wainwright Leon, *Time Out, Art and the Transnational Caribbean,* Manchester, New York, Manchester University Press, 2011.

Walker John A., *Left Shift, Radical Art in 1970s Britain*, London, New York, I.B.Tauris, 2002.

Williams Raymond, *Culture and Society,* (1958), New York, Columbia University Press, 1983.

Williams Val and Susan Bright (eds.), *How We Are, Photographing Britain from the 1840s to the Present,* London, Tate Publishing, 2007.

Zabunyan Elvan, *Black Is a Color,* Paris, Dis Voir, 2004.

Printed by

PETRO OFSETAS

Lithuania

EUROPE

September 2016